"In his teaching, preaching, and writing James Bacik has explained Christ's revelation and grace to many. This book is a personal system arranged around central topics moving from the spiritual life to the church facing new challenges. Here, ideas and words, reflecting the author's ministry to parish and university, emerge from pastoral creativity and personal experience. The reader finds faith and church drawn into the future."

Thomas F. O'Meara, OP
University of Notre Dame

"This book is the result of the love for a great theologian and the skill of a great teacher. James Bacik demonstrates beautifully how rich the thought of Karl Rahner is for spirituality and pastoral practice and how an authentic spirituality and ministry has roots in the best of theology. Written in a deceptively simple style, *Humble Confidence* provides nourishment and inspiration for beginning students of theology, for seasoned pastors, and for veteran scholars alike."

Stephen B. Bevans, SVD
Louis J. Luzbetak, SVD, Professor of Mission
and Culture
Catholic Theological Union

"Karl Rahner was arguably the most important Catholic theologian of the twentieth century, yet his work is notoriously difficult to grasp, given his reliance on dense European philosophy and an arcane vocabulary. In James Bacik we have a master interpreter of Rahner's theology and an extraordinary pastoral theologian. Drawing on a lifetime of study, Bacik cuts through the jargon and difficult philosophical categories to provide us with a compelling account of Rahner's creative theological vision, one that is easily accessible to the nonspecialist. Bacik is not content, however, simply to synthesize Rahner's thought; he also makes a compelling case for why Rahner still has much to offer the modern believer today."

Richard R. Gaillardetz
Joseph Professor of Catholic Systematic Theology
Boston College

"Elegantly simple and profoundly pastoral, this is a beautiful, soul-satisfying book. Bacik has a lucid grasp of Rahner's theology. He loves it because Rahner's insights have enabled his own pastoral ministry in a later American context. Plentiful examples of Bacik's creative 'Reflections' show how this interweaving happens in practice. An interesting, spiritually rich, and enlightening read."

Elizabeth A. Johnson, CSJ
Fordham University

Humble Confidence

Spiritual and Pastoral Guidance
from Karl Rahner

James J. Bacik

A Michael Glazier Book

LITURGICAL PRESS

Collegeville, Minnesota

www.litpress.org

A Michael Glazier Book published by Liturgical Press

Cover design by Jodi Hendrickson. Photo of Karl Rahner. Attempts to trace copyright have been unsuccessful.

Excerpts from documents of the Second Vatican Council are from *Vatican Council II: Constitutions, Decrees, Declarations; The Basic Sixteen Documents*, edited by Austin Flannery, OP, © 1996. Used with permission of Liturgical Press, Collegeville, Minnesota.

Scripture texts in this work are taken from the *New American Bible with Revised New Testament and Revised Psalms* © 1991, 1986, 1970 Confraternity of Christian Doctrine, Washington, DC, and are used by permission of the copyright owner. All Rights Reserved. No part of the *New American Bible* may be reproduced in any form without permission in writing from the copyright owner.

Excerpts from James Bacik, "Karl Rahner on God," in *Models of God and Alternative Ultimate Realities*, ed. Jeanine Diller and Asa Kasher (New York: Springer, 2013), 441–51. Used by permission.

Excerpts from James J. Bacik, "Rahner's Anthropology: The Basis for a Dialectical Spirituality," in *Being and Truth: Essays in Honour of John Macquarrie*, ed. Alistair Kee and Eugene Thomas Long (London: SCM Press, 1986), 168–82. Used by permission.

1   2   3   4   5   6   7   8   9

Library of Congress Cataloging-in-Publication Data

Bacik, James J., 1936–
   Humble confidence : spiritual and pastoral guidance from Karl Rahner / James J. Bacik.
      pages   cm
   "A Michael Glazier book."
   ISBN 978-0-8146-8316-3 — ISBN 978-0-8146-8341-5 (ebook)
      1. Rahner, Karl, 1904–1984.   I. Title.
   BX4705.R287B33   2014
   230'.2092—dc23
                                                    2014015857

For my friend Kathleen Marie Angel,

who types my articles,
organizes my world,
assists on my projects,
and reinforces my conviction that the Mystery is gracious

Contents

Introduction

This book has several functions. Primarily, it gathers together important spiritual and pastoral resources scattered throughout the voluminous writings of the influential German Jesuit theologian Karl Rahner (1904–1984) so that this treasure is more available to a wider audience. This valuable resource is drawn from his academic works but also from his many spiritual writings—work that is often neglected but is engaged here to highlight its pastoral significance.

The chapters that summarize Rahner's contributions to major areas of theology are composed as responses to specific Christian concerns today. This helps validate Rahner's claim that theology, when done properly, encourages spiritual development and pastoral effectiveness. The book can also be read as a response to those who claim Rahner's day has passed and that his theology no longer plays a significant role in the church. For the most part, the chapters do this indirectly and implicitly, but there are also explicit arguments for his continuing relevance. Finally, it is an expression of my gratitude to Karl Rahner for enriching my spiritual journey and pastoral practice for over fifty years. Shortly after my ordination as a priest of the Diocese of Toledo in 1962, I accidentally discovered the pastoral significance of his theology and have continued to draw on it ever since. The book title, *Humble Confidence*, represents the personal fruit of dialogue with Rahner and his theology. Rahner's work can inspire us with confidence in the power of the Spirit and the value of the Catholic tradition, while stressing our complete dependence on divine grace. Over the years I have written many articles that draw on the content and method of Rahner's theology. Some of the more recent ones are collected in this book to exemplify his ongoing contribution to an authentic Christian life.

Chapter 1 recalls some of the formative influences on Rahner and then examines his anthropology by noting general characteristics of human existence found in his philosophical and theological works. These characteristics, combined into pairs, serve as the foundation for what I call "dialectical virtues," such as committed-openness and hopeful-realism.

The second chapter summarizes Rahner's doctrine of God, highlighting the ultimately mysterious character of the Holy Mystery. There is also a brief treatment of his theology of grace that encourages reflection on the experience of the Spirit in ordinary life. Rahner's spiritual writings contain many poetic descriptions of the God who is always beyond all of our images. The chapter summarizes his wise teaching on prayer in five sections, each of which contains a scriptural and theological response to a contemporary challenge, as well as a prayer of my composition, usually a paraphrase of one of Rahner's own prayers.

Chapter 3 presents Rahner's Christology as a response to the specific challenges Christians face today in developing a relationship to Christ, such as questions of the historicity of the gospels and developments in modern science. The second part of the chapter uses some of Rahner's meditations on the life of Jesus, including his birth, transfiguration, and death, to give more concrete expression to his treatment of Christ.

Chapter 4 uses elements of Rahner's ecclesiology to respond to four challenges facing the church today: the split between religion and science; the large exodus of Catholics from their church; the proper way to interpret Vatican II; and the renewal of parish life. It includes a summary of Rahner's very significant article on the emergence of the world church.

In the final chapter, I write personally about Rahner's influence on me and my pastoral ministry in order to highlight the practical significance of his theology. Included are memories of my personal interactions with him in the 1970s, which reveal something of his personality. For the past thirty-five years, I have written a monthly

"Reflections" article on some aspect of my pastoral concerns. This final chapter contains some of the recent ones that suggest Rahner's influence on my ministry.

The book's epilogue deals directly with the charge that Rahner's theology is no longer helpful for the church today. My defense of Rahner underscores the enduring importance of the new theological paradigm he created. It also notes his continuing significance for Catholic theologians, like Elizabeth Johnson, and his budding influence in the Pacific Rim, especially in China.

Christian Anthropology: Cultivating Dialectical Virtues

The great German Jesuit theologian Karl Rahner claimed that the more scientific theology is, the more spiritually and pastorally relevant it will be. We can begin to exemplify that claim by examining some of the building blocks of his Christian anthropology as they developed in relation to his spiritual journey and academic career. Born on March 5, 1904, in Freiburg im Breisgau, Germany, he grew up as the middle child of seven in a family deeply steeped in the Catholic tradition. In that family setting, he developed a positive sense of human nature that sustained him throughout his whole life. When asked as a renowned theologian why he was a Catholic Christian, he responded that he remained a Catholic because he was born one and had found nothing better to help him understand the great questions of life and to live more nobly and responsibly. At the center of the faith that he maintained throughout his life was the intuition that we human beings are positively oriented to God.[1]

Jesuit Training

In 1922, Karl, following his older brother Hugo, joined the Society of Jesus, thus beginning a lifelong relationship with the Jesuits that would have a profound influence on his religious sensibilities. His prayerful engagement with the *Spiritual Exercises* of Ignatius deepened his intuitive sense that human beings can find God, who surpasses all our words and images, in all things, including the most mundane experiences. He saw the *Spiritual Exercises* as a valuable instrument for achieving a greater openness to the mystery and discerning the divine will.

From 1924 to 1927, Rahner continued his Jesuit training by studying the traditional scholastic philosophy in Pullach near Munich. Not content with this approach, he also read substantial parts of a five-volume work on metaphysics by the Belgian Jesuit Joseph Maréchal, who introduced him to the transcendental approach to philosophy practiced by Immanuel Kant. Maréchal accepted Kant's emphasis on the input of the knower in the knowing process but placed this subjective factor in the context of the dynamism of the human spirit that actively searches for the truth that always exceeds its grasp. Rahner appropriated this fundamental notion that human beings have an unlimited drive for truth and later expanded his sense of the dynamism of the human spirit to include the unquenchable desire for a love that is satisfying and imperishable.

Even when immersed in philosophical study, Rahner's theological interests were never far from his mind, as some of his early spiritual writings suggest. For example, in 1932, he published in French an article on the spiritual senses in Origen.[2] A year later he addressed the same topic in the thought of Bonaventure, showing in both studies that human beings have the fundamental capacity to know something of the always mysterious God.[3]

Influence of Heidegger

In 1934, Rahner's Jesuit superiors sent him to Freiburg for doctoral studies in preparation for assignment as a professor of philosophy. During this time, he was admitted to the famous seminar conducted by Martin Heidegger and, in fact, was given the prestigious responsibility of taking notes for the group. I recall a private conversation with Rahner in 1976 when he played down the influence of Heidegger on his theology, by sternly reminding me that Heidegger did not write about important theological topics like Christ and the church. Rahner's early philosophical works, however, are clearly influenced by his teacher, as is his general theological method and his treatment of particular theological issues, such as the meaning of death. In an article written in 1940, "The Concept of Existential Philosophy in Heidegger," Rahner highlights themes of special interest to him from Heidegger's *Being and Time*.[4] He is taken with Heidegger's method of inquiring about being in its totality by analyzing the a priori conditions necessary for human existence in the world. This analysis uncovers general structures of human existence that Heidegger calls "existentials." Human beings find themselves thrown into the world subject to a restlessness unsatisfied by any particular reality. Human existence is temporal, a movement toward the ultimate boundary of death. We human beings have the root power of free self-disposal, of taking up an attitude toward our given situation in the world. Rahner recognized that Heidegger's own analysis moves toward a radical atheism, but he was also convinced that a more complete and deeper examination of human existence could be profoundly religious and open to a possible divine revelation.

Rahner's philosophical and theological works follow the Heideggerian methodology of searching for ultimate reality through an analysis of human existence in the world, especially the a priori conditions that make knowing and loving possible. In his early philosophical works, Rahner follows his teacher's method by analyzing human beings as capable of unrestricted questioning, and in his theological writings he often begins with human experiences that can be correlated with Christian doctrines. This methodology grounds Rahner's bold assertion that the experience of self is the experience of God. Furthermore, he makes use of Heidegger's existentials to describe human existence in the world: for example, that we are historical beings moving toward death. To Heidegger's list, he adds the supernatural existential, our fundamental God-given orientation to the Holy Mystery. Rahner's studies with Heidegger convinced him that the turn to the subject in modern philosophy could be used to disclose the spiritual dimension of human existence and to ground a theology open to the contemporary world.

Study of Aquinas

In pursuing his doctorate in philosophy, Rahner wrote a dissertation on the metaphysics of knowing according to Aquinas. He explored in depth the Thomistic thesis that it is impossible for humans to know anything without an imaginative element, which Aquinas called "turning to the phantasm" (*Summa Theologiae* I Q. 89). Rahner interpreted the treatment of knowing in Aquinas from the perspective of the transcendental philosophy he appropriated from Heidegger and from Kant through Maréchal. At the same time, he went to great lengths to show that his interpretation was faithful to Aquinas, who had already recognized a subjective element in human knowing. This effort did not satisfy Rahner's supervisor, Martin Honecker, who rejected the dissertation as too influenced by modern subjectivism. Despite this harsh judgment, Rahner published the work in 1937 under the German title *Geist in Welt*.

Spirit in the World

Rahner's rejected dissertation, published in English translation as *Spirit in the World*, provides an insightful phenomenology of human questioning. Human beings necessarily question and cannot finally evade the question of being in its totality. The question about being has a transcendental dimension since it includes calling human existence itself into question. From the transcendental perspective, we appear as creatures open to the whole of reality, in contact with being without being able to master it. We can question because we are already with being in its totality, but we continue to question because being as such eludes our total grasp. In asking about being as a whole, we are already in contact with the goal of our inquiry, while our continual questioning means we are finite creatures limited by the world of time and space. Thus we are in the presence of being not as disembodied souls but only as bodily creatures dwelling on this earth.

Rahner contends that the dynamism of the human spirit necessarily involves a pre-apprehension or a co-apprehension of being. This suggests that being is co-known in every act of knowing some particular being. In analyzing knowing, we can ask about the nature of self-transcendence and the scope or extent of the goal toward which it tends. Rahner argues that the goal cannot be a finite reality or a particular object, since it exceeds every effort to define or master it. The goal of human transcendence is, rather, the infinite that makes all knowing possible. The infinite goal cannot be directly grasped in itself but is co-known in every apprehension of individual objects. Human knowing is possible only on the condition that the goal of our spiritual striving is open to the whole of all possible objects. We know individual things only within the horizon of being as a whole and in the process have an unthematic or implicit knowledge of being itself.

In his early philosophical writing, Rahner used the Latin term *esse*, translated as the act or power of existence, to point to the goal of human transcendence that is more than all possible things and is the infinite power that makes all particular things actual. Only if being is infinite can it serve as the condition of possibility for the existence of any particular thing. For Rahner, being is not only the sum of all things known and knowable; it is, rather, the infinite power beyond all that human beings can know and comprehend. From this perspective, we see ourselves as spirit because our inner dynamism is oriented to a goal that is absolutely infinite. On the other hand, we are finite spirits because we cannot directly grasp the absolute as a possession but can only co-know it indirectly as the horizon of our questing spirit. In short, we pre-apprehend the infinite in all of our acts of knowing.

For Rahner, being as the act of existence cannot be a mere regulative ideal or an impersonal force or sheer nothingness. This treatment of human transcendence and the dynamism of the human spirit demands the activity of a source and a goal that actually exists. His phenomenology of human questioning and his metaphysics of knowing discloses the existence of being in its totality. At the end of his long metaphysical study of knowing, Rahner describes human beings as spirit in the world, finite creatures with infinite longings, who are "in the world and on the way to God." We are "the midpoint suspended between the world and God, between time and eternity."[5] With these explicitly religious formulations, Rahner set the stage for his effort to develop a philosophy of religion and a contemporary theology.

Hearers of the Word

Rahner's second major philosophical work, *Hearers of the Word*, repeats some of the major themes from *Spirit in the World*: the luminosity of being that reveals its intelligible structure and essential unity with knowledge; a metaphysical anthropology that emphasizes the dynamic drive of the human spirit for being as a whole; and the hidden aspect of being that always exceeds our grasp. Rahner expands these familiar themes with less explicit reference to Aquinas and with greater freedom in identifying absolute being with God. Rahner sees *Hearers* as a contribution to a philosophy of religion that prepares for a theology of revelation. He wants to demonstrate that human beings are fundamentally open to a possible revelation from God. To do this, he moves beyond the cognitive categories of *Spirit in the World* and analyzes human beings from the viewpoint of freedom and love. Through a free decision, we are called to accept our position in the world as finite creatures before an infinite Creator. Freedom is our root capacity to take up an attitude toward ourselves and our most important relationship to God. Freedom is not merely stringing together a series of good or bad decisions; it is, rather, the essential ability to determine ourselves in our totality as persons. As Rahner puts it, "freedom is the capacity for the eternal," the root power to make ourselves to be what we will be forever. Our task is to get our desires in proper order, to direct our decisions to what is truly good, and to orient our will to God. For Rahner, metaphysical anthropology can arrive at the conclusion that human beings stand in free love before the God of a possible revelation. As free creatures, we are called to overcome the temptation to direct our desires and longings in destructive directions that will narrow the horizon of our openness to being as such. We must stay open to whatever content God wishes to communicate to us and to whatever method the Holy Mystery may employ to instruct us.

Rahner's philosophy of religion puts great emphasis on the concrete, bodily, and historical dimensions of human existence. We apprehend the material world through our senses, and our knowledge always contains an imaginative element. As finite beings, we are embodied spirits immersed in a world of time and space. Human beings can actualize themselves and determine their relationship to the absolute only through a succession of decisions over a period of time. Thus, a metaphysical anthropology, developed from a transcendental perspective, can arrive at the conclusion that human beings are essentially bodily, historical beings.

With this conclusion established on philosophical grounds and not simply as an empirical fact, Rahner goes on to argue that human beings, in order to be faithful to their nature as spirit in the world, must listen for a revelation of the true God that can only occur through human words uttered in historical experience. Human beings, structured by a spiritual dynamism and immersion in the material world, can only hear a potential word of God in concrete history and in no other way that bypasses the finite world. Rahner recognizes that God is free to speak a word to human beings in their history or to remain silent. A philosophy of religion rooted in his metaphysical anthropology can only show the possibility of divine revelation. It is the further task of theology to examine whether such a word has ever been spoken in human history.

Rahner's two early philosophical works generated a great deal of commentary. Reacting to some telling criticisms, close colleagues of Rahner urged him to rework this material. Although Rahner did not do so himself, he did allow Johann Metz, his student and friend, to make revisions to both *Spirit in the World* and *Hearers of the Word*, subsequently giving his approval to the results. For his part, Rahner moved from philosophy into the world of theology, devoting the rest of his life to teaching and writing in that field.

Philosophical Criticisms

Questions remain about the relationship between Rahner's earlier philosophical works and his later theological writings. Some critics find deficiencies in his metaphysics of knowledge and contend that they undercut the validity of his whole theological enterprise. Others see flaws in his philosophical anthropology but argue that his vast theological corpus stands as an independent achievement with its own inner logic and coherence. Friendly commentators tend to assess the philosophical works more positively, and look for organic connections between his transcendental philosophy and his innovative reinterpretation of traditional Christian teachings. For me, the key to relating his philosophy and theology is found in his notion that faith is the highest achievement of reason. Rahner clearly did not think of philosophy as a neutral search for truth without presuppositions. His metaphysical anthropology and his philosophy of religion were not intended as an independent foundation for doing theology. In both his metaphysical and theological writings, Rahner gave expression to his faith conviction that we human beings are oriented to absolute mystery. The early philosophical books attempt to vindicate this conviction through a transcendental analysis of human knowing and loving, while the later theological writings explain and apply this faith stance in the light of Christian doctrine.

Toward a Christian Anthropology

Many of Rahner's spiritual insights are rooted in his theological anthropology. He never produced an integrated and comprehensive Christian anthropology, but his philosophical writing and his vast theological corpus are filled with insightful descriptions of human existence that help fill out his fundamental intuition that human beings are positively oriented to the infinite. In developing his anthropology, Rahner sometimes speaks with Heidegger of "existentials," which are formal general structures or characteristics of human existence. On other occasions, he simply describes various aspects of human nature or particular ways in which individuals experience themselves. It is possible to identify at least fourteen of these existentials scattered throughout his writings, which can then be organized into seven dialectical pairs.[6]

1. The first thing to be noted about human existence is that we are persons and unique subjects. Our personhood is implied in our essential orientation to God. It directs our attention back to this primordial relationship, which grounds all particular relationships. While we are tempted to understand ourselves merely in terms of external causes, the term "person" reminds us that we are called to take up an attitude toward all external factors. In this experience, we are conscious of ourselves as unique individuals who are greater than the mere sum of what empirical studies reveal about us. This is not a statement about one aspect of human existence but indicates that we confront ourselves as a whole and experience our subjectivity as the a priori condition of every particular experience. We are responsible for ourselves and experience ourselves as subjects when we analyze our motives and behavior.

2. We are self-transcendent beings, which suggests that we experience ourselves as striving to move beyond all limits while always searching for something more. We know this aspect of our existence

especially in our ability to reach out to others in love as well as in our frustrated searches for the perfect lover or the love that is imperishable. However, we must remember that this existential points not merely to a particular experience, no matter how painful or exhilarating, but to our a priori openness to being in general, which forms the background for all individual experiences. In speaking of ourselves as self-transcendent, we are not referring to a particular type of activity that proceeds from one part of us called the "soul," but to the fact that we human beings as a whole are driven and allured by a power greater than ourselves.

3. We are knowers with an unlimited drive to understand but with finite capabilities. This means that human knowing involves, on the one hand, an infinite questioning, a transcending of all particular knowledge and a dissatisfaction with partial answers; and on the other, an immersion into the particularity of this world, a need to think in limited concepts and images and an inability to comprehend reality as a whole. As knowers we experience our growth in knowledge and understanding as an invitation to expand our experiences, to deepen our insights, and to improve our judgments.

4. We are called to live in a responsible freedom, which means that we are unavoidably accountable for our lives as a whole. This points to a fundamental characteristic of human existence, in which we have the power to decide about ourselves forever. Freedom is not merely a neutral capacity to choose among alternatives, nor is it simply the power to revise or reverse decisions. It is rather the capacity for the infinite, the power to do something of permanent validity, to make ourselves to be what we will be forever. Despite all determinisms in life, human beings have the power to take up an attitude toward themselves and thus assume responsibility for the totality of their existence. As free creatures we are a single unified process of self-actualization through which we determine our eternal destiny.

5. We are historical creatures immersed in the world of time and space. Our existence in the world is not an accidental addition to our transcendence but precisely the situation through which we actualize ourselves. Our historicity means that we find ourselves thrown into a world both of persons and things that have a power to shape our

consciousness and determine our existence. At the same time, we are called upon to create our world, to use our time constructively, and to influence history. In all of this process we cannot escape the limitations implied in our creaturehood, our bodiliness, and our immersion in the rhythm of time. Our situation in life is always influencing and limiting our free disposal of ourselves. Any effort to live in total self-sufficiency or in a pure subjective interiority can only lead to frustration.

6. Human beings remain radically threatened by guilt and sin. Although we possess our existence from a power outside ourselves, it is still possible for us to be unfaithful by saying "no" to that infinite source that we call "God." Thus it can be said that the threat of personal sin is an abiding existential of human existence. In addition, sin and guilt codetermine the very situation in which we must freely actualize ourselves, so that in Christian terms we can speak of original sin as an existential that influences the whole of human history, although it is always surrounded by a more powerful grace. Thus there is in us a division or a self-alienation resulting from the fact that our freedom can never totally master or integrate all the elements that are given to us prior to our free decisions. While parts of an individual's personality are the product of free decisions, there is much that remains impersonal, unilluminated, unaffected by personal decision. Rahner calls the resulting split or lack of integration "concupiscence," which suggests we never become wholly absorbed either in good or in evil.

7. Human life is necessarily communal and social. We can only achieve authentic existence in relationship with other people. Self-realization and personal relationships grow in like and not inverse proportion. Our social orientation is not simply a secondary addition to our individual nature but a constitutive dimension of our very existence. It is possible to specify this point by distinguishing certain dimensions in our communal life: as bodily creatures, we are related to a biological community or environment; as spiritual beings, we are related to various personal communities, such as family, neighborhood, and state; as religious persons we are related to a church; and as individuals incorporated into Christ we are related to the whole human family.

8. We are the creatures who move inevitably toward death. Death should not be thought of merely as a biological event in which we are passively struck down by a force outside ourselves. It is rather a spiritual act by which we freely hand over our lives to the gracious mystery. Thus death is not just the separating of body and soul but our great opportunity to ratify the general orientation of our lives toward the good and thus to reach our final fulfillment. Death appears to us as the final boundary of our lives, but the eyes of faith also discern it as the passageway into eternity. We know death not only as a future event but as an abiding reality that touches our daily existence. Within life we must live with death by accepting our creaturehood with all of its possibilities and limitations.

9. Personal existence survives biological death. We are called to a final eternal fulfillment of all of the deepest longings of our heart. Eternity is not a very long linear continuation of time but rather the ultimate validity of our spiritual freedom that comes not after death but through it. Thus we live with eternity in time as it shines through our experiences of generous love, steadfast fidelity, and inner peace. It is precisely because we already know the hints of eternity in our lives that death is so threatening to us. Our deepest hope is that love is stronger than death and that our efforts in life have a final validity. Faith, which is expressed as belief either in the immortality of the soul or the resurrection of the body, grounds this hope and enables us to discern the intimations of eternity in ordinary life.

10. Human persons are sexual beings. This does not refer simply to the generative faculty but to a quality that affects all aspects of human existence and partakes in our essential relationship to the absolute mystery. In other words, sexuality stamps our whole personality and is reflected in all our activities. It propels us out of ourselves and moves us to seek union with others. We relate to one another as males and females and actualize ourselves through these relationships not by abstracting from sexual differences but precisely through them. Furthermore, it is in and through such loving human relationships that individuals achieve and manifest their love of God.

11. Human beings always remain dependent on the past, both as members of the human race and as individuals. The communal aspect

of this dependency results from our necessary immersion in an inter-personal world and extends to the very origin of humanity that con-tinues to influence the whole of human history. In addition, we are dependent on our own past, since our exercise of freedom in the present is conditioned both by previous decisions and also by the elements in our nature that have escaped integration through free decisions. If we are to live wholeheartedly in the present, we must accept our past by celebrating our successes and transforming our failures. The past is a rich resource for self-understanding and self-improvement.

12. We are the beings who are responsible for creating our own future. This essential aspect of our nature has only emerged into consciousness in modern times with our increased ability to control our destiny. This phenomenon raises the question of our hopes and our relationship to the future. To a certain extent we can plan our-selves and shape our future. The future toward which we are directed, however, is ultimately not simply our own finite creation but is the work of God, the gracious One, who draws us into the future.

13. We are the beings who in order to fulfill ourselves must go out of ourselves into the world and must reach out in love to other human beings. This is not just a matter of psychological wisdom but a propo-sition of theological anthropology, which maintains that human exis-tence is structured in such a way that we can only actualize ourselves through interaction with our environment and especially other human beings. We are interdependent creatures who need others so that we can break out of the prison of selfishness and experience the liberation of caring for others. In turn we perform an important ser-vice for others by being receptive to their love.

14. We are the ones who, in order to achieve genuine fulfillment, must return to ourselves. To avoid self-alienation and a scattered piecemeal existence, persons must be quiet and turn inward in a process of self-discovery. We must attempt to order and integrate the vast amount of experience flowing from our encounters with the world of persons and things. Again, this is not simply a question of psychic health but an essential characteristic of the spiritual creature. In fact, for Rahner, a being is spiritual precisely to the degree that it

is able to accomplish the return to self or, in other words, to achieve self-presence. As finite spirits immersed in the world of matter, we have the power to step back and return to self in a process that makes human knowledge and all spiritual activities possible. It is in this achievement of self-presence that we actuate ourselves and demonstrate our distinctively human characteristics.

Organizing the Existentials

In examining Rahner's anthropological insights, it is difficult to find a way to organize the material in a coherent fashion while being faithful to its rich diversity and complexity. Some have chosen a key category, such as "person," or "man of mystery," or "self-actualization," as the organizing principle. In the *Foundations of Christian Faith*, Rahner himself provides a theological ordering that describes successively human beings as persons, transcendent beings, responsible and free, historical, dependent creatures oriented to mystery, beings threatened by sin and guilt, and finally, as the event of God's self-communication. Rahner did not intend this as a comprehensive theological anthropology but as the basis for his theological reflections and as a limited contribution to a much-needed contemporary expression of the general characteristics of human existence. I find it more in tune with contemporary experience in the Western world to organize his statements about the fundamental structures of human existence into pairs of opposites that are dialectically related. For example, the proposition that human beings are individuals can only be properly understood when it is related to the statement that human existence is necessarily communal. This approach seems to me to be faithful to Rahner's own fundamental outlook, which appreciates the complex pluralism of human existence and recognizes the impossibility of surveying that pluralism from a simple organizing principle. On the other hand, Rahner does not favor simply setting two apparently opposed characteristics side by side without determining their fundamental relationship. Rather than settle for a simple juxtaposition, he is interested in determining the primordial unity of related entities. Applied to our attempt to organize Rahner's anthropological insights this means that we should not merely pair dialectically opposed statements but also show how they ultimately flow from our essential nature as related to the mystery that envelopes and grounds our existence.

Dialectical Pairings

With this in mind, we can propose the following schema as a way of organizing the Rahnerian existentials.

1. We are the actively self-transcending beings who achieve our fulfillment precisely by accepting our contingency and submitting ourselves throughout our lives and in the act of dying to the Gracious Mystery.

2. We are unique individuals with an enduring, immortal, spiritual nature who can only realize our individuality by living out our communal nature in various personal communities. Both our individuality and our communal nature are rooted in our partnership with God, which we share with all other human beings.

3. We are spiritual beings who transcend all particular objects in a movement toward the infinite; and at the same time we are physical, sexual, historical beings immersed in the world of time and space who can only move toward the infinite in and through finite realities. We are finite, embodied spirits, dynamically related to the infinite mystery.

4. We are personal subjects who as a unified whole transcend all the particular elements that make up our nature; and at the same time, we are beings who are threatened by the self-alienation of sin and guilt, and who are unable to unify completely the disparate elements in our nature. Our personhood flows from our relationship with the Deity, while our alienation is rooted in our inability to respond fully to the divine summons to partnership.

5. We are infinite questioners and receptive knowers who only achieve the fullness of knowledge in a free loving response to the absolute mystery. Knowledge and the freedom implied in genuine love are both rooted in a primordial unity or personal center from which we respond freely and with awareness to the ultimate source of our being.

6. We determine ourselves and shape our future, but only under the influence of prior determinations supplied by the history of humankind and our own previous free decisions. We interact in the present with particular realities influenced by both our dependence on the past and our anticipation of the future. Ultimately, our temporality is rooted in our dialogue with the gracious God who is the dynamism and the goal of human history.

7. We are the ones who can only take possession of ourselves by reaching out to other people and things. Conversely, we can function effectively in the political or social sphere only out of a rich interior life. As unified creatures we can fully actualize ourselves only through a twofold movement of going outside of ourselves drawn by the absolute mystery, and returning to ourselves sustained by that same mystery.

Spirit in the World

When we examine these pairs of opposites, it seems possible to combine them into two comprehensive statements that are also dialectically related. Thus, on one side, we have all the characteristics that involve openness and dynamism: we are spirit, self-transcendent, individual persons, the infinite questioners, free and immortal. On the other side, we find the traits that reflect some type of limitation: we are at the same time contingent, communal, material, finite, historical, sexual, temporal, concupiscent, and subject to death. If we use the word "spirit" to summarize the first group of characteristics, and "world" the second, we arrive at Rahner's own characterization of human existence as spirit in the world. "Thus, we are," he writes, "the mid-point suspended between the world and God, between time and eternity, and this boundary line is the point of our definition and our destiny."[7] Of course, "spirit" and "in the world" are not just two existentials accidentally related. They imply each other and one cannot exist without the other. The finite spirit must become sensibility and be immersed in the world if it is to realize itself.

If we can summarize the existentials in the dialectical phrase "spirit in the world," then we must still make sure it is understood in terms of our essential relationship to the absolute mystery. We are properly understood as spirit in the world only when we realize that our encounters with the absolute mystery come precisely in and through finite reality.

A Dialectical Spirituality

Rahner's dialectical anthropology provides us with a solid and comprehensive basis for working out an approach to the spiritual life that fits the experience of persons in the contemporary Western world. Today so much of the spiritual struggle is to bring apparently opposite and competing tendencies into an integrated system. At our best we strive for a wholeness that refuses to negate authentic aspects of our human existence. A theological anthropology that recognizes the danger of collapsing one or the other competing poles and celebrates the ideal of a lifelong quest for integration is a valuable resource indeed for today's spiritual journey.

A contemporary dialectical spirituality that is rooted in current experience and in a solid anthropology celebrates a distinctive set of ideals. These ideal characteristics can be expressed in terms of paired opposites in order to reflect our lifelong struggle for integration and to suggest the hidden, often paradoxical, connections between the polarities. Without going into great detail, let us examine some of these ideals or contemporary virtues.

Committed-Openness

We must guard against both a mindless relativism, which judges one position to be as good as another, and a narrow exclusivism, which tries to monopolize truth and goodness. Instead, we need a free and intelligent commitment to our particular standpoint, which in turn will enable us to pass over with confidence to the standpoints of others in a search for meaning and value greater than we now possess. For example, we should strive to root ourselves so firmly in our religious tradition that we possess the confidence to be open to truth and goodness wherever it is found. A commitment to our religious heritage, which is based on a genuine understanding and appreciation of both its strengths and weaknesses, is precisely what will enable us to enter into a fruitful dialogue with other traditions.

Reflective-Spontaneity

In our culture we are in danger of falling into either an excessive and paralyzing introspection or a superficial, unexamined immersion in the activities of life. Our ideal instead should be to combine a spontaneous immersion in the present moment with periodic self-examination, which in turn frees us to live more fully in the now. We want to live in a self-forgetful way, but this requires self-examination. It is desirable to be attentive to our current experience, but this seems to be facilitated by regular meditation. Our goal is to participate wholeheartedly in the events of our lives, but we need insight and understanding to do so. We need to find a proper frequency and method for our reflective times so that they don't increase our anxiety and preoccupation with self but rather help free us to listen to the God who speaks to us in the present moment.

Hopeful-Realism

Our culture seems to present the temptation to swing from a naïve optimism to a cynical pessimism as ideals are tarnished and dreams unfilled. In reaction we must strive for a spiritual maturity that is in touch with reality, including its dark and tragic dimension, but that maintains a lively confidence in the ultimate triumph of good over evil. At the same time, we must be aware of the signals of hope in our everyday experience that remind us of God's final victory over suffering.

Enlightened-Simplicity

Some people find themselves fixated in a childish religious outlook that ignores the ambiguity of life and runs on emotion divorced from reason. Others are trapped in a pseudosophistication in which a little bit of knowledge has obscured the whole point of authentic religion. We ought to avoid these tendencies by striving for a spirituality that includes a purity of heart founded on an adequate theology, a humble charity based on insight, an uncomplicated lifestyle intelligently chosen, and an utter dependence on God matched by a creative use of our talents. We want to have an adult understanding of our faith but one that recognizes it as the simple good news that there is a gracious God who loves us despite our unworthiness.

Prayerfully-Prophetic

It is not uncommon today to find people very serious about prayer but lacking concern for the needs of the oppressed and disadvantaged. On the other hand, some people, serious about improving our world, find prayer irrelevant to that task. To avoid such one-sidedness, it seems important to develop a prayer life that intensifies our awareness of social injustice and moves us to prophetic action on behalf of those oppressed. At the same time, involvement in the struggle to humanize our world should send us back to prayer where we recall our dependence on God and seek new energy and strength for the struggle.

These characteristics of a dialectical spirituality are not exhaustive and obviously need further explanation and exemplification. However, they do set a tone, map a direction, and indicate a task. I believe there are growing numbers of people who find this dialectical approach closer to their experience and a more reliable guide in their quest for meaning, commitment, integration, and a richer human life.

Spiritual Writings[8]

In his homilies and prayers, it is clear that Rahner's anthropology does not derive merely from a philosophical analysis of human existence but is rooted in the Christian conviction that we are hearers of a saving word from the Lord. In *Prayers and Meditations*, Rahner recognizes that we are a "frightful puzzle" to ourselves and "no amount of questioning" can fathom the depths of our relationship to "the God of free favors." Like Augustine, Rahner understands the restless heart. "We are all pilgrims on the wearisome roads of our life. Every end becomes a beginning. There is no resting place or abiding city. Every answer is a new question. Every good fortune is a new longing." Responding to the Freudian emphasis on the power of our unconscious inner drives, Rahner claims that the "writhing coil" of our cravings really points to "a thirst for infinity," which our Creator placed "in the very depths of our nature." It takes eyes of faith "to see behind and through all these dark forces a much more powerful force—the power of the presence of the Holy Spirit."

In his insightful book *The Love of Jesus and the Love of Neighbor*, Rahner rejects "an autonomous anthropology," which leads to the individualism that plagues Western society, in favor of "a communion anthropology," which recognizes the solidarity of the human family and the interdependent character of human existence. This anthropology views love of neighbor as "a sacred inexorably enjoined duty" that is always "embraced and borne up by the absolute mystery of the infinite God." A Christian anthropology has "the improbable optimism" to assert that "average human beings" who "ply their way through life" can rise above "the miserable narrow anxiety of their existence" and "the banality of everyday life" by loving others in simple unselfish acts of kindness, understanding, and compassion. By "daring to risk" our own autonomy and freedom in genuine acts of love, we enter "into the unfathomable, unbounded dwelling place of God."[9]

Rahner's Christian anthropology, which highlights our orientation to mystery and our essential interdependence, will continue to provide spiritual searchers in the twenty-first century with a valuable alternative to the self-contained humanism and the excessive individualism so prevalent in our culture.

2

Doctrine of God:
Deepening Our Prayer Life

Rahner's understanding of God reflects the influences we have already noted: his experience as a Catholic believer and his training as a Jesuit priest; his studies with Martin Heidegger; his examination of the metaphysics of knowledge in Aquinas; his philosophy of religion; his Christian anthropology; as well as his reinterpretation of traditional Christian teaching on grace, Trinity, revelation, salvation, and Christ.[1]

Reason and Faith

In developing his doctrine of God, Rahner did not accept a sharp distinction between philosophy and theology or reason and faith. He rejected both the Enlightenment ideal of reason as a detached neutral instrument and the popular notion of faith as a personal conviction immune from critical examination. For him, philosophy always contains a secret or implicit theological dimension, as long as it is true to its own inner dynamism and does not arbitrarily restrict its search for wisdom. Reason is unavoidably influenced by social conditions and cultural assumptions, as well as personal interest and bias. For Rahner, genuine faith is not opposed to reason but is its greatest accomplishment and highest achievement. Reason is true to itself when it recognizes its limitations before the mystery of being, and faith is authentic when it accepts the mystery as caring and loving. Faith is not an irrational feeling or an arbitrary opinion; it is a conviction that must vindicate itself as genuine knowledge through a process of critical reflection. This intrinsic dialectical relationship between faith and reason, as Rahner saw it, is crucial to understanding his approach to the doctrine of God.

Rahner initially approaches the question of God through his anthropology, which sees human beings as essentially oriented to mystery. We cannot know God directly but only as the Source and Goal of the dynamism of the human spirit. Our drive for knowledge and love implies a quest for absolute truth and love. Theology as doctrine of God grounds and completes anthropology. Our treatment of human existence in chapter 1 sets the stage for this chapter on God.

Mystery

In his theological works, Rahner typically uses the word "mystery" to refer to the source and goal of the dynamism of the human spirit. He opted for this term because it calls for further reflection and carries a more inviting tone than the traditional language of being. Referring to the goal of human transcendence as mystery reminds us that it is not a particular being or object contained within our time-space coordinates. The goal must remain nameless, undefined, and, in principle, not subject to limitation. We know mystery precisely in knowing ourselves as self-transcendent creatures with longings that always exceed our apprehension and grasp. When Rahner examined our drive for a love that is totally fulfilling, he referred to the goal of this longing as the "holy mystery." We know the gracious character of mystery through a transcendental reflection on the giving and receiving involved in loving personal relationships. Christian faith affirms that the Holy Mystery does not remain distant and uncaring but draws near as a loving personal presence, most fully realized in Jesus Christ, the Word made flesh.

Foundations of Christian Faith

Rahner's most comprehensive theological work is *Foundations of Christian Faith*, designed to present Christian belief as a whole without attempting to explain every aspect of it or answer all objections to it.

The first two chapters of *Foundations* repeat many of the ideas from his philosophical writings but place them in a more explicit theological context. After an introduction that explains his methodology and deals with epistemological problems, the first chapter presents an anthropology with Christian overtones. Human beings are persons who can have a loving relationship with God. We are finite creatures, responsible before the Creator for ourselves as a whole. Our transcendence is lived out in historical experience where our origin and ultimate goal remain hidden from us. In all our human striving, we remain dependent on the ineffable mystery that encompasses us.

The Word "God"

In chapter 2 of *Foundations* we find Rahner's developed doctrine of God.[2] It is a reflection on our transcendental experience of encountering the absolute mystery. We only know what the word "God" means by reflecting on our fundamental orientation to mystery. In this reflection, anthropology and theology are united, forming a solid basis for his contention that the experience of self is the experience of God. He begins his reflection with a linguistic thought experiment. What would happen to human beings if the word "God" disappeared from our vocabulary without a trace or an echo? We would then be unable to reflect on our lives as a whole and to seek the ultimate meaning of our existence. We would not realize that the deepest questions had faded from our consciousness, and, therefore, we would revert "to the level of clever animals."[3] In fact, the word "God" does exist, kept alive by believers as well as by those who deny God's existence. We ourselves do not create the word "God." On the contrary, it comes to us as a gift in the history of language. Rahner finds some truth in Ludwig Wittgenstein's famous admonition to remain silent about things that cannot be expressed clearly. For Rahner, God is "the final word before wordless and worshipful silence in the face of the ineffable mystery."[4]

Knowledge of God

After showing how the word "God" functions by keeping open the great questions of identity and meaning, Rahner examines at length what kind of knowledge we have of God.[5] He rejects as illegitimate the common practice of forming a concept of God and then asking if this being exists. He insists that we can only know anything about God by reflecting on our transcendental experience of mystery. For Rahner, there is no natural knowledge of God, as the manualist theology claimed, but only a supernatural knowledge rooted in the graced character of our transcendental experience that is always mediated by concrete historical realities.

God and World

Assessing two of the common ways of understanding the relationship between the world and God, Rahner finds an element of truth in pantheism, since it is open to God as the primordial ground and the ultimate goal of transcendence. He is harsher in his criticism of a naïve theism that portrays God as a supreme being who stands over against created reality. This kind of dualism, which shares some of the assumptions of popular atheism, is in danger of making God into a being among others and of misinterpreting the inner dynamism of the world.[6]

Rahner opts for a God who is distinct from the world as its creator and yet is intrinsically present as its divine energy. This God remains mysterious, indefinable, and ultimately beyond all measure. This position reflects Rahner's linguistic point that the word "God" does not function like other words signifying individual objects or events within our temporal-spatial world. It points, rather, to the source and goal of our longings that cannot be contained within our limited frame of reference.

Proofs

In exploring what we can know about God, Rahner takes up the question of the validity and function of the traditional proofs for God's existence. He denies that these proofs provide new previously unknown knowledge of God and rejects the traditional claim that they can demonstrate the existence of a first cause or most perfect being that we call "God."[7] The proofs function, rather, as a secondary reflection on our primary transcendental knowledge of God. Each of the five traditional proofs found in Aquinas highlights some aspect of our experience that points to the Holy Mystery. Rahner suggests that individuals seeking to vindicate their faith should reflect on their most meaningful and revealing experiences: for example, the capacity for absolute questioning; overwhelming anxiety; the joy that passes all understanding; and the sense of an absolute moral demand.[8] These experiences all reveal a transcendental relationship to mystery. In them, we know ourselves as finite and we co-know God as our intrinsic dynamism and as the ultimate goal beyond our control. The proofs attempt to name the mystery co-apprehended in the deeper experiences of life. They make explicit the fundamental structure of human existence that is dynamically oriented to the ultimate goal we call "God."

Analogy

Continuing his discussion of God, Rahner returns to an analysis of religious language, especially the traditional idea of analogy.[9] He rejects the popular notion that analogical language stands midway between univocal and equivocal language. For him, analogy is rooted in our essential condition as human beings, who know particular things against a horizon that cannot be comprehended in categories drawn from this world. Not only is language necessarily analogical, but, more fundamentally, we exist analogically, oriented to mystery that surpasses all the categories, symbols, and words derived from our worldly experiences.

Rahner detects an unavoidable tension in all efforts to speak about God. Our language always falls short, inadequate to the task of speaking about the Holy Mystery. Traditional scholastic theology made a similar point by insisting that our language about God is more unlike than like the Holy Mystery. Rahner applies his notion of analogy to the statement that God is a person. This does not mean that God is an individual center of consciousness, like a human being who is separate from all other humans. It does mean that God cannot be reduced to an impersonal cosmic principle or an unconscious ground of being. God is a person in the sense that we can have a personal relationship to the Holy Mystery that includes worship and prayer.

Dependence on God

In our temporal experience as infinite searchers with finite capabilities, we know ourselves as creatures.[10] For Rahner, creation is not merely an event that occurred billions of years ago but an ongoing process by which God sustains the world and all human beings in historical existence. We are totally and radically dependent on God, who always remains free in relation to the finite world. Rahner claims that the more we realize and accept our dependence on God, the more we experience true freedom. In this regard, human beings face two types of temptations: either to shift our proper responsibility for ourselves onto God or to act autonomously, without recognizing or accepting our dependence on God. We achieve true freedom by resisting these two temptations and accepting our total dependence on the Holy Mystery that empowers us to act freely.

Finding God in the World

In the last section of his treatment of God in *Foundations*, Rahner takes up the issue of finding God in the world.[11] Religious traditions, including Christianity, speak about God in categorical terms: for example, intervening in history, working miracles, and inspiring sacred books. Rahner thinks that many people today who are comfortable relating to the ineffable mystery in general are put off by the concrete claims of religions that God has acted in specific ways in history. His fundamental response to this concern is that God is present to the world through a "mediated immediacy."[12] This means that God's presence in the world as its origin, goal, and inner dynamism is always accomplished in and through particular finite realities. In scholastic terms, God acts in the world not as an external efficient cause but as a type of formal or intrinsic cause.

Religious claims of God's specific activity in human history are attempts to make explicit the transcendental presence of God in the whole world. Aquinas made the same point by insisting that God works through secondary causes. God causes the world and the chain of casualty we observe in it; but God does not insert the divine presence as a link in that chain. Religious claims about divine interventions in history are really faith statements based on the concrete manifestations of God's abiding presence in human history. To illustrate this point, Rahner asks how to interpret the origin of a good idea that comes suddenly to an individual and proves to be correct, valid, and helpful. It is possible to trace the idea back to psychological factors, previous experiences, lingering memories, and other finite causes. At the same time, believers, who freely accept their dependence on the Holy Mystery, can also legitimately claim that good ideas are inspired by God and say a prayer of gratitude for them. Rahner sees no reason why believers cannot extend this explanation to all the good things that happen in life, so that, as he puts it, they are seen as "an inspiration, a mighty deed, however small, of God's providence."[13]

Grace

Rahner expanded his doctrine of God by reinterpreting the traditional teachings on grace and the Trinity. From the Greek fathers of the church, especially the great seminal thinker Origen, he retrieved the fundamental notion of uncreated grace.[14] The Holy Mystery gives to human beings not a created reality but the very divine self. God is both the Giver and the Gift. The divine self-communication created the world and continues to sustain its evolving development. It brought human beings into existence and guides the historical process. God's self-giving found its fulfillment in Jesus Christ, the perfect respondent, and will reach its ultimate goal at the end time when God completes the process. The Christian God is not remote but draws near in loving intimacy. God's self-giving divinizes us, makes us temples of the Holy Spirit and incorporates us into the Body of Christ.

Rahner was critical of certain developments in the theology of grace in Western Christianity. Contrary to Augustine's salvation pessimism that spoke of large numbers who are damned, Rahner emphasized a salvation optimism based on the power and omnipresence of uncreated grace. He insisted that just because grace is a free gift does not mean it is rare. On the contrary, divine grace informs, sustains, and guides the whole evolving cosmos and all aspects of human existence. We live and move and have our being in the divine milieu.

The whole world is indeed "charged with the grandeur of God," as the Jesuit poet Gerard Manley Hopkins put it.

Experience of Grace

Popular Catholic piety in the United States, influenced by the Baltimore Catechism, tended to view grace as a kind of supernature sitting on top of our natural being, out of the range of our normal everyday consciousness. Rahner, echoing the integrated theology of Aquinas, insisted that grace penetrates and transforms human nature.[15] To say grace is supernatural means that it is totally gratuitous—not that it is extrinsic to human nature. God is not removed from consciousness but is the condition present in all our knowing and loving. Thus Rahner's theology of grace confirms the conclusion of his philosophy of religion that God is co-known in all individual acts of knowing and, by logical extension, co-loved in all acts of love. This sets up the spiritual imperative that we must always be on alert for clues to the divine presence, for glimpses of the Spirit, and for intimations of the Gracious Mystery. Once again, the experience of self is the experience of God. All things are potentially revelatory. Everything that constitutes our human existence can speak to us of God.

Our experience of grace is often paradoxical, grounded in our ability to see light in the midst of darkness. There are degrees of religious experiences based on our closeness to God and on our ability to reflect on our experience of the divine presence and to express it accurately. History and culture affect our perception of the presence of the Spirit. Some experiences are more effective catalysts for spiritual insight than others. In our culture today, for example, personal relationships and the burden of freedom seem to have a special power to evoke a sense of the mystery dimension of life. We can distinguish two general types of spiritual experiences: boundary or limit experiences, such as failure and death, which remind us of our total dependence on God; and ecstatic experiences, like deep joy and intimate love, which suggest the gracious character of the mystery that always surrounds us. All of our attempts to speak about our experience of divine grace are always limited and incomplete. God is always beyond all our words and images. For Rahner, following Aquinas, God remains incomprehensible even in the beatific vision. In heaven, we encounter the inexhaustible love of God.

Mystagogy

Rahner's theology of grace alerts us to the abiding presence of God in all aspects of our daily lives. In our secular world, however, God's presence is often eclipsed by the busyness of life and the cares of this world. Human existence can become one-dimensional, lived on the surface with little sense of the depth dimension. We can become totally caught up in legitimate, preliminary concerns while neglecting matters of ultimate concern. Sensitive to this challenge of the secular age, Rahner advocated what he called "a mystagogical" approach to pastoral ministry and spiritual development.[16] Borrowing this term from classical liturgical texts that refer to initiation into the sacramental life of the church, he applied it to the effort to initiate people today into a deeper sense of the mystery dimension of life. The mystagogical task is to help individuals interpret correctly their deeper experiences, achieve a greater conceptual clarity of their deeper experiences, and find a proper symbolization of their religious experience. Recognizing common human experiences is the first step in a process of relating the Christian tradition to contemporary life. Contemporary theology, for example, has reinterpreted the classic Christian understanding of salvation to include various forms of liberation from demonic forces operative in this world, but this has current relevance only if people are aware of the ways in which the secular world can imprison us in destructive habits of mind.

Mystagogical Practices

Pastoral leaders can employ many different ways of opening up the mystery dimension of life. Dialogue with science on the immensity of the expanding universe, for instance, can remind us of our own limitations in mastering reality and our dependence on a much larger power. Language that is vivid, colorful, and poetic has a power to disclose the mysterious depths of human existence. While technological, scientific language promotes mastery of the material world, "evocative language" exercises power over us, alerting us to the presence of the infinite in the finite. Rahner highlights the mystagogical function of "primordial words," which originate in the deep experience of persons and cannot be defined in terms of better known words. His favorite example is the word "heart," which indicates the center point of the human person, a place of unity, deeper than the split between body and soul, where we encounter God. Centering prayer makes use of primordial words, like "heart," "peace," and "love" to promote inner harmony and receptivity to the Spirit.

Mystagogical Passages

Rahner's writings contain many "mystagogical passages" with an intrinsic power to evoke mystery. At times he will insert a more concrete image in the middle of an abstract theological analysis. For example, in the introduction to *Foundations of Christian Faith*, while discussing transcendental experience, he suddenly introduces a concrete image, comparing our accumulated knowledge to a small floating island, illumined by the light of science, which is borne by the sea. The image raises the question of what we love more, the small island of our scientific knowledge or "the sea of infinite mystery."[17]

Rahner's spiritual writings are filled with poetic passages that challenge superficial explanations of human existence. In his book *On Prayer*, he describes our inner life as "a writhing coil of cravings and blind possibilities." He warns us not to give too much power to these dark forces, making them "idols which dominate our lives." The depths of our inner life, "the strange infinites within us," are not "pools of stagnant bitterness but the waters of infinity springing up to eternal life." Here we have a vivid description of the destructive tendencies in our own soul transformed into a greater consciousness of the mysterious presence of the Holy Spirit in the depth of our being.[18]

In assessing his daily routine, Rahner sees his soul as "a bomb-pocked highway" filled with "countless trivialities, much empty talk and pointless activity, idle curiosity and ludicrous pretensions of importance." He blames himself for this state of his soul; he has dug this rut himself, transformed even holy events "into the grey tedium of dull routine." And yet he comes to see more clearly that the path to God "must lead through the very middle of my ordinary daily life." Only God's love can transform the dull routine of life into "a hymn of praise."[19] Rahner's descriptions of daily life are a form of what the psychotherapist Abraham Maslow called "rhapsodic communication." In trying to explain peak experiences, Maslow found that an abstract description of such experiences made little impact on his audience, but if he shared with them a vivid description of an actual peak experience, many individuals would be reminded of a similar experience in their own lives. Rhapsodic language tends to resonate. Pastoral leaders charged with the mystagogical task do better when they speak about the spiritual life less abstractly and more concretely.

Rahner and Nature

A transcendental mystagogy finds its completion in a categorical mystagogy that makes explicit connections with traditional Christian piety. In reflecting on nature, Rahner admitted that it was hard for him to appreciate the beauty of the created world.[20] He thought it was "the numbness of my spiritual faculty" that kept him from "going into raptures" over oceans, snowcapped mountain peaks, and the evolving universe. With obvious regrets, he confessed that he cannot "instinctively feel" the true glory of divine creation. His response to this perceived spiritual limitation was to join himself to the prayer of "that chorus of poets" who extoll the power and splendor of God's creation. Thus he prays in the style of the *Canticle of the Sun*, the great hymn of St. Francis of Assisi, trying to make his own one of the great classic statements of the way the beauty of this world serves as a ladder taking us to the Source of all beauty.

Echoing Francis, Rahner begins by praising our "sister sun" who gives us light and is the "very image" of the exalted God. His praise of God extends to moon and stars; to wind, air, and cloud; to water, fire, and mother earth. Reflecting on his prayer, which does not come naturally or instinctively from his heart, Rahner concludes that joining our prayer with those more attuned to the divine presence is a spiritually wise practice that can expand our awareness of the Spirit. It is fascinating to see Rahner wrestling with his own spiritual limitations. For him, praising nature in the style of Francis is an experiment in mystagogy. Will the rhapsodic language sharpen his appreciation of nature as home to the Spirit? Rahner certainly thought it was worth a try. His advice to us is that praying in the words of others is a legitimate practice that is surely heard by God. At the end of this experiment, he returns to the more fundamental truth that we should pray in the form and style that feels comfortable to us.

Odd Discernment

Authentic religious experiences often involve an "odd discernment" of the surprising presence of the Spirit. Rahner offers many odd descriptions of experiences where persons act according to their conscience without any real hope of earthly reward or even personal satisfaction: for example, choosing to be silent and not defend ourselves against an unjust attack; forgiving a person even though they take our action for granted and offer us nothing in return; obeying the will of God that leads to no earthly advantage; making a sacrifice that was unnoticed, thankless, and gave us no inner sense of satisfaction; persevering in the love of God without any emotional payoff; and doing an act of kindness for someone that elicits no expression of gratitude and leaves us feeling empty. Rahner goes on to say that if we have known any of these experiences, then "we may be sure that the Spirit was at work within us," and eternity encountered us in that brief moment. Such encounters with God remind us that our personal significance transcends worldly wisdom and that certain challenges in life can be faced with an "unbounded confidence" quite removed from worldly wisdom.[21]

Effective Mystagogues

Rahner urges pastoral leaders and spiritual directors to see themselves as mystagogues who can help others appreciate the mystery dimension of life. In preaching, teaching, and counseling, mystagogues help those they serve come to a more explicit understanding of the often hidden presence of the Spirit at work in ordinary life. This requires empathy for individuals who find deeper reflection difficult and even frightening, as well as for those consumed by worldly concerns.

Effective mystagogues are able to speak about common human experience in ways that resonate with ordinary people. They are good listeners, attentive to the concrete ways that parishioners talk about their joys and hopes, as well as their failures and disappointments.

When parish leaders do their mystagogical work well, parishioners often say things like: "You have expressed clearly what I have felt vaguely"; or "You must have heard our family discussion." One of the highest predictors of homily effectiveness is the statement "the preacher understands my heart." Mystagogical preaching opens up the mystery dimension of life and shows how the Scripture readings illumine and guide the deepest questions of life. They offer diverse descriptions of the human adventures, including the distinctive experiences of both women and men, both young and old, and persons of both homosexual and heterosexual orientation.[22]

Pastoral leaders can learn from the field of phenomenology how to construct descriptions of common experience that resonate with a wide variety of parishioners. Sensitive mystagogues stay open to the full range of human experience, describing significant aspects fully and accurately in search of the presence of divine grace. This means paying attention to the way people express their conscious dreams for a life filled with meaning, purpose, and commitment, as well as their emotional reactions—such as joy and anxiety—that accompany their everyday life in the world. Mystagogical effectiveness is tied to the ability to detect and use important symbols that capture and illumine significant spiritual experiences. Putting these insights from phenomenology into practice, a preacher commenting on a passage from the book of Jonah might speak of the "Jonah syndrome" as a way of symbolizing the common temptation to escape from God and to evade responsibilities, which often produces a vague anxiety. People who can identify with Jonah are more receptive to the positive Christian message that following God's will is the path to freedom.

Rahner's theology of grace helps fill out his doctrine of God by insisting that the ultimate Goal of human aspiration is not remote but draws near as the loving Source of our spiritual dynamism. The presence of the Holy Spirit within us grounds the spiritual imperative to stay alert for clues to divine grace sustaining and guiding our everyday lives.

Trinity

Rahner's doctrine of God also incorporates a critique and a reinterpretation of the traditional Western theology of the Trinity, which typically began with a discussion of the existence and attributes of the one God and then moved to examine the three persons in God.[23] Rahner preferred the common Eastern practice of beginning with the distinctive ways we relate to each of the three persons constituting the Trinity. He was also leery of Augustine's psychologizing approach, which claimed to know something of the inner life of the Trinity, commonly expressed as the Father speaking the Word and their mutual love spirating a third person, the Holy Spirit. Finally, he warned against simply repeating the traditional teaching that there are three persons in one God because in the modern world this leads to the heresy of tritheism and the popular perception that there are three gods. Rahner began his treatment of the Trinity with the threefold way we experience God in history and then applied this to the inner life of the Trinity. He expressed this approach in the axiom "the economic Trinity is the immanent Trinity."[24] By knowing how God relates to us in the economy or history of salvation, we know something true about the inner life of God. Christian tradition speaks of the one God in a threefold way: the Holy Spirit, who lives within us and serves as our Advocate; the Word or Son, who became man and walked this earth; and the Father, who sent the Spirit to animate us and sent the Son to liberate us. We experience the one God as the Source of our being and call God "Father." We are influenced by God incarnate in Jesus of Nazareth and name God "the Word or Son." We are blessed by God's gifts and speak of God as "Holy Spirit." According to Rahner, this threefold relationship to God corresponds to a real threefold difference within God. Again, the economic Trinity is the immanent Trinity. This approach frees us to develop a trinitarian monotheism and to speak of God as a communion of love. God shares the divine life with us, encouraging us to form relationships of loving mutuality and respect. Christ calls us to share in his community-building mission of spreading the reign of God. The Spirit summons us to a communion of love where justice and peace flourish and to a life of worship and prayer where we respond to divine blessings.

Spiritual Writings

Rahner's doctrine of God, often poetically expressed in his spiritual meditations, insists on the ultimately mysterious character of the One who is beyond all words and images. The incomprehensible God is the "nameless Beyond behind all that is familiar to us," the "infinite Enigma that conceals all other enigmas."[25] And yet Rahner can pray to the inexhaustible One in familiar terms: "Thanks to Your mercy, O Infinite God, I know something about You not only through concepts and words, but through experience." Grateful for meeting God in joy and in suffering, he articulates the profound truth: "You have seized me; I have not grasped You." Rahner continues his prayer: "I can never forget You, because You have become the very center of my being."[26] As a representative of the long tradition that recognizes the limitations of religious language, Rahner provides a critical challenge to the fundamentalism that claims direct access to God and detailed knowledge of the divine will. Furthermore, Rahner's consistent emphasis on the ultimately mysterious nature of God provides a solid foundation for the postmodern impulse to name God in various ways without *pretending to exhaust the divine reality.*

Summary

Throughout his whole life, Karl Rahner maintained the faith conviction that we human beings have a positive orientation to God. In an effort to explain and defend this belief, he made use of both philosophy and theology, convinced that faith is not opposed to reason but is its highest achievement. His early philosophical works offered an initial vindication of his faith in God by demonstrating that being as a whole is co-known in every act of knowing and that human beings are open to a possible revelation from God in history. His theology of grace makes the case that the Holy Mystery is not remote but lives within us, guiding our spiritual journey. His reinterpretation of the doctrine of the Trinity reminds us of our threefold relationship to the one God, the Father who creates and sustains us, the Son who saves and liberates us, and the Holy Spirit who animates and guides us.

Cultivating Our Prayer Life

Rahner's doctrine of God provides a solid foundation for the Christian practice of prayer. For him, prayer can be grasped as meaningful only in its actual practice. Prayer is a fundamental act of human existence that "must be its own justification and advertisement." It is the central religious practice that acknowledges our complete dependence on the triune God. Rahner wrote many scholarly articles about prayer and once described his book *On Prayer* as one of the best statements of his theology. At the same time, he often insisted that what we say in prayer is far more important than what we say about prayer. Prayer addressed to God involves a relationship that remains ultimately mysterious.

Some of Rahner's important material on prayer can be summarized in the following five dialectical pairs. Each pairing contains a contemporary challenge to authentic prayer, a theological perspective, an example from the prayer life of Jesus, and a prayer of my composition, usually a paraphrase or rewording of one of Rahner's own prayers.

1. Prayer lifts our minds and hearts to the God above and fosters familiar conversation with the God within. Our challenge is to develop a more mature prayer life that retains a childlike confidence in the Father who loves us. Rahner's theology reminds us that God is both the transcendent Mystery that rules the universe and the intimate Presence that sustains and guides us. The gospels tell us that Jesus committed himself totally to the will of the God who sent him to establish the kingdom and, at the same time, addressed the sovereign Lord as "Abba," the familiar term, like Daddy or Papa, used by children for their fathers.

~

Thank you Abba for revealing Yourself to me in my everyday experiences of joy and suffering. You have taken the initiative and become the true center of my existence. May I remain ever mindful of this great gift.

2. Prayer is both a gift and an expression of our freedom. According to Rahner, our challenge is to avoid a false pride that sees our prayer as a personal accomplishment and a paralyzing quietism that absolves us of all responsibility to develop a viable prayer life. Scripture tells us that the Holy Spirit prays in us, enabling us to address God as Father, which reminds us that all prayer is a gift. At the same

time, we are free persons, called to responsible cooperation with the Spirit in the process of responding to the God who calls us by name. Jesus received the Spirit at his baptism by John in the Jordan River. This Spirit drove him into the desert where he prayed in preparation for his battle with Satan. During his ministry, he prayed for individuals and shared his healing Spirit with them. Faithful to the Spirit, Jesus freely accepted death on a cross and in the process became life-giving Spirit for the whole human family.

$\sim$

I must stop the busy routine for a moment and address words of praise to You, Holy Spirit, living within me. I adore You as the Light that illumines my dark moments, the Compass who guides me along the path of moral decisions, the Hope that sustains me when stalked by despair, the Love that propels me out of selfishness into life-giving relationships, and the Power that enables all my prayers. Help me recognize and praise You as the Gift of my life and the Source of my being.

3. Prayer involves a unity of interior sentiments and external expressions. Some of us say prayers regularly and struggle to mean what we say, while others have a rich interior life that remains unexpressed. We are enfleshed spirits and our bodies are symbols of our souls. To achieve integration, we strive for a fruitful interplay between inner sentiments and external gesture, at the same time accepting the inevitable gap between the two. The quest for a totally authentic prayer life inevitably finds us disappointed, as Rahner, the sober realist, reminds us. Ideally, we gradually come to a greater realization of our total dependency on the God who rules our lives, and find more helpful ways of improving our prayer lives: for example, learning various meditation techniques, finding the best places and times for private prayer, and participating wholeheartedly in liturgy. Jesus lived constantly out of his Abba experience of total intimacy with God, which energized his complete dedication to the cause of God and humanity. He expressed and deepened this fundamental relationship by participating in the great Jewish feasts

and by carving out private prayer time in the midst of his demanding ministry.

God, sometimes the demands and responsibilities crowd out my awareness of Your constant presence. Please make my meditation time more fruitful so that I am more mindful throughout my busy day that I am never alone but always carried by Your loving embrace. Help me to learn from Your Son and my Lord to walk always in Your presence and to find time and place to nourish my spirit.

4. Prayer is both private and communal. A growing number of believers today find comfort and solace in prayerful reflection but are not comfortable praying in groups or in formal liturgy. Some regular churchgoers have difficulty finding connections between liturgical prayer and their private devotional life. Rahner insists that we are essentially social beings who grow as persons in and through various communities, including the family, intermediate associations, and the local church. We meet God in the sanctuary of our hearts as well as the church sanctuary. In prayer, we have the opportunity to encounter Christ our brother and to participate in the life of his body, the church. Our moments alone with God should prepare us for public worship, and communal prayer should nourish our spiritual life. The gospels, especially Luke, tell us that Jesus sought opportunities to engage in private prayer and prayed before key decisions, like calling his disciples. Jesus also appreciated the value of communal prayer as suggested by his participation in formal Jewish worship and by his request that the disciples pray with him during his Agony in the Garden.

Gracious God, O Lord, when we share in the eucharistic meal Your Son comes to us as our nourishment and we become what we eat, the Body of Christ. May what we celebrate in the sacred liturgy always be enacted in the daily witness of our everyday lives with its mix of hard work and moments of prayerful reflection.

5. Prayer includes adoration and petition. Some Christians have to admit that most of their prayers are devoted to asking God for things they desire for themselves or others, while rarely offering prayers of praise or thanksgiving to God. Other Christians who have grown to reject crude notions of an intervening God now find themselves questioning the value of petitionary prayer. This problem demands a more extensive treatment, especially since Rahner's doctrine of God has helped create this difficulty. Prayer is a form of truth telling that gives expression to the fact that we are totally dependent on a Power greater than ourselves. All that we are and have is a gift. Prayers of praise to the Lord of the cosmos and gratitude to the Giver of all gifts gives expression to these fundamental truths. As Rahner put it, prayer of adoration is "the last moment of speech before silence," the final reflection before abandoning ourselves to the Gracious Mystery beyond all comprehension. Moreover, it is God who makes our prayer of praise possible, empowered by the Spirit who lives within us and instructed by Christ who invites us to give glory to our Father. The regular practice of prayer not only gives expression to our sense of dependency but helps strengthen and intensify it. In and through this process, we develop our true freedom and a proper sense of responsibility for ourselves as a whole. From this perspective, prayer appears as essential to our own spiritual growth. Liturgical prayer is not simply a device for community building but an essential act of communal worship offered to God, who can be addressed as our Father through Christ and empowered by the Spirit.

Divine Intervention

Questions about petitionary prayer arise from Rahner's doctrine of God, which challenges the popular notion that God intervenes periodically in human affairs in response to requests from faithful people. For Rahner, God cannot intervene now and then because God is always already present in the whole of human history as the Source and Goal of all human activities. The gracious One is always on the side of good in the struggle against evil, always present to us as the Power that sustains and guides us. The God who raised Jesus to life never abandons us and always supports us. Through his paschal mystery, Christ is present to all people in all places and all times as the absolute Savior and definitive Prophet. The Holy Spirit anoints all people and not just a select group of believers. Divine grace is omnipresent like the air we breathe. The human opportunity and task is to cooperate with the God who wants good for us, to follow the example of Christ who planted the seeds of the final victory over evil powers, and to tap the power of the Holy Spirit who is our Advocate in the ongoing struggle against demonic forces. Rahner warns us not to think of the sufferings of life as a divine punishment for our sins or as a test of our virtue. When afflicted, it is natural to ask why but far more beneficial to ask how: How can we cope with the inevitable sufferings of life, trusting that God is with us and for us in the great struggle against all the dark forces?

A Defense of Petitionary Prayer

Within this theological framework Rahner offers a vigorous defense of petitionary prayer. The Hebrew Scriptures, especially the Psalms, are filled with explicit petitions, asking God for specific help. In the gospels, Jesus urges his disciples to ask for divine favors with great confidence that the Father hears our prayers. He taught us to pray the Our Father with its petitions for daily bread, forgiveness for sins, and deliverance from temptation. Jesus himself responded to faith-filled requests for healing. In offering prayers of petition, Rahner reminds us to begin by surrendering to God's will, as Jesus taught us in the Lord's Prayer. "Thy will be done" precedes "give us this day our daily bread." A proper surrender of will means: letting go of the desired results and not making an idol out of what we desire; overcoming the temptation to manipulate God or achieve a magical result; and recognizing that our prayer might be answered in different ways than we envision.

After surrender to God's will, we can place ourselves before God with all our concrete needs, desires, fears, and burdens. This is not an inferior form of prayer. In a way it involves a type of praise by recognizing that God is the true source of all blessings. Petitions involve a healthy sense of call and response, since God first speaks to us, calling us by name in the very act of sustaining us in life. By raising Jesus to a glorified life, God has already answered the deepest longings of our heart in the most radical way. The resurrection is the ultimate positive response to the petition that we are, expressed in our desire for personal happiness, loving relationships, and a more just and peaceful world. As Christians, we believe God is personally involved in human affairs. Rahner insists that there is an orthodox way of speaking about God changing for the sake of human beings, as happened in the incarnation, with the Logos taking on human flesh for the first time during the reign of Caesar Augustus. Rahner's notion that "God changes in the other" sets a framework for thinking about the dynamics of petitionary prayer, without relapsing into a crude interventionist notion of divine providence.

One Human Family

As members of the one human family of God, we are all connected by bonds that are deeper and more significant than all the differences that divide us. Christ died and rose for all people, and the Holy Spirit animates and unites the whole universe and all the inhabitants of spaceship Earth. As interconnected persons, we have the power to influence one another. Sometimes the influence is perceptible: for example, when a young Pakistani girl speaks up for the importance of education for women and continues the crusade after being shot in the head, we all benefit. We can imagine an African American high school student praying for the Pakistani girl and in the process finding motivation to go to college herself. Another example: a husband prays for reconciliation with his wife after a serious dispute. His prayer moves him to apologize and her to accept his overture, leading to a reconciled relationship, an answer to prayer. Many times, however, the causal connections engendered by petitionary prayer are not evident, but this does not mean that no connections exist. We can assume that the deep relationships forged by the Spirit among all human beings enable some transfer of positive energy between individuals and groups, however mysterious the process might be.

Prayers for others in need and for worthwhile causes operate on that assumption, trusting that the Spirit works for the good of all.

Prayer and Miracles

Rahner insists that effective petitionary prayer does not involve a miraculous breaking of the laws of nature. For him, miracles are signs of the presence of the reign of God, as John's gospel makes clear. Miracles occur when individual believers detect the hand of God at work in a special way in particular events. The material world is open to spiritual energy. The laws of nature contain more potential developments than scientific inquiry currently recognizes. In petitionary prayer, we are not asking for God to break the laws of nature but for the gift of openness to the often surprising power of the Spirit.

Practically, prayer of petition has important positive consequences: reminding us of our complete dependence on God and our personal limitations; alerting us to problems in the world as when we pray for people starving or suffering from local wars; moving us to constructive action to help ourselves and others; and opening our minds and hearts to greater cooperation with God's grace in the great task of humanizing our world.

~

Gracious God, I adore You as the Lord of the stars. I praise You as the Source of all beauty. I worship You as the Fulfilment of my longings. I thank You as the Giver of all good gifts. I put before You my prayers for a peaceful heart, loving relationships, and a just world. I realize these are gifts from You and that I must cooperate with Your grace in pursuing them. All my words of adoration and petition seem so feeble. They seem to float off into empty space. Please help me persevere in lifting my mind and heart to You.

3

Christology:
Betting Our Lives on Jesus

Rahner's Christology is a powerful resource for deepening our commitment to Jesus Christ as the absolute Savior and definitive Prophet. Christianity is not merely a philosophy of life or an acquired wisdom but involves a personal relationship to Christ that is never complete and always open to further growth. As Rahner put it: "I am a Christian in order to become one." We can use Rahner's vast writings on Christ to respond to specific challenges people face today in making the Lord the center of their lives.

Historicity

Beginning with a fundamental challenge, we can ask if we know enough about Jesus of Nazareth to bet our lives on him.[1] Do we have enough historical knowledge of Jesus to justify committing ourselves to him? Modern Scripture scholarship has sharpened the problem by calling into question the historical accuracy of some Gospel material. Scholars tell us the gospels are not objective biographies but rather documents of faith, written by believers in order to spread and deepen commitment to Christ. In many cases, we don't know if we have the exact words of Jesus. There are discrepancies between the Synoptics and John's gospel: for example, was the Last Supper on Passover or the day before? Some miracles appear to be legendary, like Jesus' sending demons into swine who then jump over a cliff. There is the possibility that the transfiguration scene is actually a post-resurrection event placed back into the public ministry of Jesus. These and many other questions generated by gospel scholarship are now available to ordinary believers in a popular form, creating doubts for some Christians about continuing a relationship with Jesus begun in childhood.

Modern theology has debated this challenge in terms of the relationship between the Jesus of history and the Christ of faith. How does the Christ revealed in the New Testament relate to the historical Jesus? Do we know enough about the life and ministry of Jesus to affirm the validity of the gospel witness? At one extreme are agnostic scholars who claim we can know very little about Jesus of Nazareth: for example, only that he was an itinerate rabbi who once called God "Abba." At the other extreme are those who reject modern scholarship in favor of a fundamentalist conviction that the gospels are inerrant portrayals of Jesus.

Beginning with the remarkable fact that over two billion people in the world today say they are followers of Jesus, Rahner presents various ways believers can vindicate their faith for themselves and share it with others in a credible way. As Christians, we cannot offer logically compelling proof to nonbelievers that Jesus is truly the Son of God. We can offer a coherent account of our belief and demonstrate by example that it helps us live lives of greater responsibility and love. For ourselves, we must learn to accept calmly the inevitable gap between our commitment to Christ and the available historical evidence. We do this effectively in other areas of life: for example, most of us live on the assumption that a particular man is our biological father without having absolute proof of paternity. By a similar logic, Christians live out a belief in Jesus without having absolute certitude about all the facts of his earthly life. Belief in Christ is self-validating when it helps us to understand the deep questions of life and to live in a loving way.

Rejecting both extreme agnosticism and inerrant fundamentalism, Rahner recognizes that mainline Catholic scholarship maintains that we do have a substantially correct picture of the historical Jesus. His own approach, however, bases his Christology on the single bedrock historical fact that Jesus did claim to be the absolute Savior, the One charged with establishing the reign of God in the world. The whole New Testament reflects this historic claim made by Jesus, and all four gospels attest to it in various ways. For Rahner, the resurrection makes this claim of Jesus credible. The Father raised Jesus to a new glorified life, thus validating his life as the definitive prophet. In justifying our own Christian faith, we can bypass the miracles of Jesus and concentrate on his claim to be the absolute Savior. Rahner's approach frees believers today to maintain faith in Christ without answering every problem with the historical Jesus raised by Scripture scholars.

Docetism

Some Christians today have trouble establishing a genuine relationship with Jesus because they do not accept his true humanity.[2] He is true God and worthy of worship, but it is hard to think of him as brother or friend because he is not really like us. Rahner believed that many Catholics today are implicit heretics, unable to accept the full humanity of Jesus. He calls them "crypto-Docetists," recalling the early heresy of Docetism that claimed Jesus did not have a real physical body but only the appearance of one. To prompt reflection, Rahner asks if we can affirm that Jesus shuddered before the Mystery and went to his death in darkness. Hesitancy in giving an affirmative answer to such questions suggests the need for a deeper appreciation of the full humanity of Christ.

Traditional Christology, based on John's gospel and developed in the early councils of Nicea, Ephesus, and Chalcedon, has a descending dynamism. The eternal Logos comes down from heaven and pitches his tent in our midst, as one translation of John's gospel has it. The Word becomes flesh. The Son of God assumes the complete human nature of Jesus in the hypostatic union. Although the essence of this union was never officially defined, there is a proper exchange of attributes so that we can legitimately say the eternal Son of God died on the cross and the son of Mary rose from the dead. For Rahner, this traditional "from above" or descending Christology has the enduring value of safeguarding the divinity of Jesus so that he is not reduced to one of many provisional prophets or religious geniuses. On the other hand, the mere repetition of the traditional formula of Chalcedon, that Jesus is one person with two natures, human and divine, can lead to a denial, at least implicitly, of his full humanity and true human personhood. Simply saying Jesus is God without nuance or explanation can lead to the heresy of monophysitism, a denial of the full humanity of Jesus.

In order to overcome the limitations of Chalcedon, Rahner developed an ascending or "from below" Christology that begins with the human Jesus portrayed in the Synoptic Gospels. He is a man like us in all things but sin, as the apostle Paul put it. Jesus is born of Mary, grows up without much notice in Nazareth, is baptized by John, prays to God, gathers disciples, preaches the Good News, heals the sick, exorcises demons, remains faithful to his mission, runs afoul of the religious and political authorities, and is executed by crucifixion. He knew the full range of human emotions, including joy in the beauty of God's creation, frustration with his disciples, anger in the temple, anxiety in the garden, and abandonment on the cross. As Luke tells us, Jesus grew in wisdom, age, and grace, suggesting development in his consciousness of his identity and mission.

When the disciples first encountered Jesus, they were attracted by the man and his teaching but struggled to understand him in depth. Only after the resurrection did they come to a full realization of his true identity as the Son of God. Taking seriously the synoptic perspective, Rahner sees Jesus as a fully human person who was so open to the divine presence and so responsive to the divine call that it is true to say he was God personally present in our midst.

Consciously and actively, Jesus freely accepted God's self-giving love totally and completely. Throughout his life, he remained faithful to his role as the absolute savior charged with establishing God's reign in the world. When he met with failure, he had to revise his approach, but always in fidelity to the divine will. He did not seek suffering but accepted it as the byproduct of meeting his responsibilities. Faithful to his mission, he disregarded the warning of the disciples and went to the capital city of Jerusalem where his enemies arrested him. In his agony in the garden, he prayed to be spared the anticipated suffering but, as always, in the context of choosing his Father's will. Despite his feeling of abandonment on the cross, Jesus freely handed himself over to his Father.

This portrayal of Jesus in the Synoptic Gospels provides fertile ground for an ascending Christology that highlights the humanity of Jesus. For Rahner, Christology is the fulfillment of anthropology. Jesus is the best that the evolutionary process has produced. He is our model of the human person fully alive, completely actualized, and totally loving. Rahner insists that this approach denies nothing of the traditional descending Christology and implies the fundamental Christian teaching that Jesus is the Son of God. As an alternative orthodox approach, ascending Christology has the great advantage of challenging implicit Docetism, while enabling all of us to identify more completely with Jesus who is truly one of us.

Christ in an Evolutionary Framework

Some people today find it difficult to relate to Jesus because their modern scientific worldview clashes sharply with the static world of the Bible. To them, the claim that God came down from the heavens above, lived briefly on this earth, and then returned to heaven sounds mythological. Jesus seems like a Hindu avatar who appears briefly in human history only to soon disappear. Keenly aware of the challenges created by modern science, Rahner developed what he calls "a transcendental Christology," that presents the incarnation of the Son of God as an intrinsic possibility within an evolutionary view of the world.[3] In this Christology, God is the Source and Goal of the one, unified, material-spiritual evolving world. Rahner speaks of matter as "frozen spirit" with the intrinsic possibility of developing toward spirit, eventually leading to human beings, who are inspirited bodies, or enfleshed spirits.

Our evolving world is the result of God's self-communication that created the big bang some 13.7 billion years ago and has continued to guide and sustain the evolving universe ever since. As the material evolving world became more complex, it became more open to spirit and consciousness. The evolving world became conscious of itself when human beings arrived on the scene. Humans now play the role of cooperating with God in the ongoing creation of the world. Historically, some human beings have been more receptive to God's self-giving than others. The German philosopher Karl Jaspers identified "the axial age," from about 800 to 200 BC, when especially receptive humans appeared in different parts of the earth and made important contributions to the spirituality of the human family. Jaspers' list includes Confucius and Lao Tzu in China, Siddhartha

Gautama the Buddha in India, Isaiah and Jeremiah among the Israelites, and Socrates in the Greek world. Mindful of this kind of historical development, Rahner imagines a point where divine self-giving love and a gradually deepening human receptivity meet in a person who is totally and completely open to God's grace. This person would be the absolute savior who makes definitive and irrevocable God's saving will. The dialogue between God and the human family would continue, but an ultimately positive outcome would be assured. The Christian claim is that this imagined meeting point of divine self-giving and human receptivity did actually occur in history in the person of Jesus of Nazareth.

The Incarnation

Transcendental Christology sets the stage for a categorical Christology that can take up all the traditional questions about Christ in an evolutionary framework. From this perspective, the incarnation has no hint of mythology but appears as the definitive fulfillment of the divine self-communication that is the Source of the whole process of evolution. As the incarnate Word, Jesus makes the invisible God present in our history. He is the concrete parable of the Father, the visibility of divine love, the sacrament of the Gracious Mystery.

The Christian doctrine of the incarnation asserts not only that Jesus is the Word made flesh but also that divinity and humanity remain permanently and irrevocably united in him. The resurrected Christ remains the God-man, who continues to mediate on our behalf. This reminds us of the intrinsic value of the common human nature we all share with Christ and highlights the abiding support of the Lord who shared our earthly experience of joy and sorrow.

Rahner's Christology not only clears the way for Christians today who are formed by modern science to commit themselves to Christ but also encourages a spirituality deeply rooted in the concrete physical dimension of everyday life. We grow to maturity not by being lifted out of the material world but by immersing ourselves more fully in the human condition. We make spiritual progress not by despising the physical realm but by embracing it as the divine milieu. The story is told of a little girl who is afraid ghosts are in her bedroom. She seeks comfort from her mother who assures her that there are no ghosts and that God is with her to protect her. The girl replies, "Yes, but I need someone in here with skin." As Rahner emphasizes, the incarnate Word responds to the human need for skin, for tangible presence, for a concrete form of the invisible God.

A Paschal Piety

Some Christians have a limited relation with Jesus because their piety centers exclusively on the horrible suffering he endured to save us from our sins. The popularity of Mel Gibson's movie *The Passion of the Christ* suggests the extent of this type of piety. Rahner's theology of the death and resurrection provides a broader understanding of the salvific activity of Christ that opens up the possibility of a healthier relationship to him.[4] His holistic anthropology precludes thinking of death as the separation of soul and body, involving the demise of the body and the ongoing life of the soul. Death is, rather, an activity of the whole person, our freest act that makes definitive our fundamental option for good or for evil. In death, we pass from this life to everlasting life, taking with us all that makes us unique persons, formed by the exercise of freedom throughout our earthly lives. The Bible typically speaks of the afterlife in terms of the resurrection of the body. Under the influence of Greek philosophy, Christians today often express their ultimate hopes in terms of the immortality of the soul. Rahner struggled, unsuccessfully, until the end of his life to find a way to include the resurrection of the body and immortality of the soul in a single unified statement of belief that would encompass both.

Death of Jesus

Participating fully in the human condition, Jesus freely accepted death as a byproduct of fidelity to his mission. He was not a masochist seeking suffering; he was committed to the will of God, and that brought him to death on a cross. Through his death, he brought to focus and fulfillment his whole life of loving service. On the cross, he made definitive and irrevocable the surrender to the will of God that characterized his very being. As Rahner poetically expressed it, Jesus "allowed death to swallow him into the innermost center of the world" so that he "might establish his divine life in it forever."[5] The most significant element in the death of Jesus was not the terrible suffering he endured, as some forms of popular piety have it, but rather his complete obedience to the divine will, even to death on a cross as the apostle Paul expressed it in his letter to the Philippians (2:1-12).

Resurrection

Turning to the resurrection, Rahner warns us against various false interpretations. It is not the resuscitation of the body of Jesus as he had done for Lazarus. Jesus was not simply raised in the subjective faith of the disciples as the Protestant New Testament scholar Rudolf Bultmann claimed. The resurrection is rather the validity of the life and message of Jesus and the vindication of his claim to be the absolute Savior charged with establishing the reign of God. Rahner's approach encourages us to look to the resurrection for other positive messages: God is totally trustworthy, faithful to the divine promises; Jesus is indeed the definitive Prophet; the Holy Spirit transcends death; death is not the last word but paradoxically leads to new life; love is not foolish but is stronger than death; grace is more powerful than sin; the final salvation of the world is assured.

From a pastoral viewpoint, Rahner advises us to proclaim the resurrection in the context of the human desire for ultimate meaning and for a love imperishable. The resurrection enables us to believe what we desperately hope is true, that all of our good actions have a permanent validity and that none of our efforts to love others are ever wasted. As Christians, we are baptized into the paschal mystery, sharing in Christ's death and resurrection. We have died with him and we shall live forever with him—that is our hope. The fact that billions of people throughout history have professed belief in Jesus, a man who knew so much failure and rejection, is indeed remarkable in itself. Applying Rahner's imagery, the resurrection is like "the first eruption of a volcano" indicating that God's loving fire is "in the interior of the world," already embracing many and primed to bring all things into the divine light.[6] I like to think of the resurrection as a second big bang, releasing an inexhaustible spiritual energy into the world that sustains and guides not only Christian believers but all human beings. When shared with others, this energy is not diminished but multiplied. Ultimately it will triumph over all the dark forces in the world. Through his death and resurrection, Christ has created a vast reservoir of spiritual energy that assures the final victory of good over evil.

Rahner's theology of the paschal mystery puts commitment to Christ in a positive light. We can relate to him not as a revered figure from the past but as the living Christ present to us today across all barriers of time and space. We can follow Christ not merely as one who suffered terribly but as the Lord who won the victory over suffering and death. Discipleship involves dying to self but always for the sake of a new, more vibrant life in service of the reign of God.

Traditional Soteriology

Some Christians who accept Christ as their savior are uncomfortable with popular ways of explaining his saving work. Classic soteriology as developed by Anselm of Canterbury (d. 1108) held that human sins were infinite because they offended the infinite God. Only Jesus as a divine being could offer the necessary infinite satisfaction to God for the sins of mankind. At a popular level this satisfaction theory tended to make God into an angry tyrant who demanded that Jesus suffer horrible torment to make up for offenses against the divine majesty.

Rahner offers an alternative explanation of salvation designed to highlight God's universal love and Christ's role as representative of the whole human family. The story of the human race, always a mix of grace and sin, is really a single unified history, despite all its diversity and fragmentation. That history is created by a dialogue between human beings and the gracious God, who wills to speak a definitive word of love to the human family. God's offer of himself can be definitive only if accepted in an irrevocable way in the act of dying. Jesus, as the exemplar of perfected humanity, represents the whole human race. His death, freely accepted, made irrevocable his lifelong commitment to do the will of God. Resurrection, as entrance into glorified life, is not the result of a divine judicial judgment but simply what happened organically when Jesus emptied himself totally and surrendered himself completely to God's love.

Rahner summarizes his theology of salvation: "We are saved because this man who is one of us has been saved by God."[7] As a result, the loving God has made his desire to save all people present in our world "historically, really, and irrevocably."[8] For Christians uncomfortable with the notion of Jesus as the victim of divine displeasure, Rahner offers a theology that stresses God's abiding love and Christ's free commitment to the cause of God and humanity. As Christians, we commit ourselves to Jesus not as a passive victim of divine wrath but as the faithful one freely accepting death on a cross as a passage to risen life.

Christian Exclusivism

Christians interested in dialogue with world religions need a way to combine their personal commitment to Christ with an openness to the truth, goodness, and beauty in other religious traditions.[9] Christian exclusivism maintains that divine revelation is confined to the Bible and church teaching while other religions are untrustworthy products of human origin. For Catholics, the Second Vatican Council ruled out this option by making positive statements about world religions as genuine vehicles of grace and truth and by encouraging interfaith dialogue. Reacting strongly against such exclusivism, recognized theologians like John Hick and Paul Knitter have insisted that major religious traditions like Judaism, Hinduism, Buddhism, and Islam are genuine vehicles of grace apart from any direct connection with Christ.

Rahner holds a position between these two options based on his conviction that Christ, as the absolute Savior, must be the prime guiding and sustaining presence operative throughout the whole history of salvation, which began with the first humans and will be complete only at the end of human history. This dynamic presence is manifest in the world religions and reaches its definitive highpoint in Christianity. The God who wills the salvation of all people communicates the divine self to the whole world, creating a universal revelation and the possibility of saving faith for all who follow their conscience. Thus Rahner can speak of an anonymous Christianity present in other religious traditions and of anonymous Christians who live out Gospel values without an explicit reference to Jesus. He recognizes that these terms should not be used in actual dialogue with other believers and that they could be offensive. On the other hand, he insists that they express the traditional Christian view that all grace is Christic. As an aside, Rahner said he would gladly accept being called an anonymous Buddhist by someone complimenting him for exercising the kind of compassion enjoined by the Buddha.

In interreligious dialogue, Rahner advised using the language of spirit, a suggestion that has influenced Catholic participants. Christ is operative in other religions through his Spirit. Christians believe the Spirit, who was at work in the whole history of Israel and was a guiding force in the life and ministry of Jesus. The Spirit that came upon Jesus at his baptism guided him to a desert retreat and sustained him in conflict with Satan. Through his death and resurrection, Jesus became life-giving Spirit for all people at all times. This same Spirit was at work in the influential religious prophets and spiritual masters such as Moses, Confucius, Siddhartha Gautama, and Muhammad. Christians can enter into dialogue with the world's great spiritual traditions, confident in their commitment to Christ and therefore open to ways his Spirit is operative in other religions.

Personalistic Language

Some Catholics are generally uncomfortable with talk of a personal relationship with Jesus. They may associate this language with evangelical Protestantism and people who speak boldly about accepting Jesus in their heart as their personal Savior at a particular moment on their spiritual journey. As a young man, Rahner preferred more sober expressions of his commitment to Christ. Only later in his life, as he himself tells it, could he speak comfortably about "throwing his arms around Jesus in an act of love."[10] The fact that a great theologian continued to grow in his faith is itself instructive for those struggling to avoid complacency and deepen their faith. On the other hand, there are Catholics who are as uncomfortable with Rahner's language as they are with evangelical expressions. Perhaps they will eventually be more at ease with such personal expressions of faith. In the meantime, they need a way of speaking about Christ that feels authentic and does not seem inferior to more emotional faith expressions.

Christ should play a central role in the lives of all Christians, a more important role than any finite reality, including the church, the Bible, other prophets, money, pleasure, power, and status. We can imagine various ways Christians might express this fundamental centrality of Christ. He is my moral Compass in a world of competing values. His life of love and service is my greatest source of inspiration. For me, Jesus is the supreme Source of wisdom. He is the Good Shepherd who guides me through the dark valley. Contemplating his death on the cross was the only thing that enabled me to deal with my father's death. Jesus is the Son of God, and I worship him at Mass. Christ is the cosmic Lord who rules the whole universe. These typical statements all express the centrality of Christ in the life of Christians. They all can be deepened and expanded, but they need not be considered inferior to more personal expressions of faith in Christ.

Reflecting on the Life of Jesus

Rahner's Christology not only clears away obstacles to faith in Christ, it also invites prayerful reflection on Jesus and his role in Christian life. His spiritual writings, especially his *Spiritual Exercises*, are extremely valuable resources for such reflection. There we find an invitation to engage Jesus in the gospels "in the way two lovers gaze at one another in the living of their daily life together."[11] In this experience, we meet the real Jesus who communicates truths to us "that otherwise we should not have known."[12] The shape of Christ's life is the norm and ideal for our own lives. Rahner invites us to engage specific events recorded in the gospels, trusting that Jesus is the standard for a fulfilled human existence. This is not an abstract analysis of a gospel passage but a faith-penetrated remembrance of specific occurrences in the life of Jesus.

The Birth of Jesus[13]

Luke's version of the birth of Jesus has captured the imagination of Christians for two millennia: a Roman census forces Joseph and his pregnant wife, Mary, to travel from their hometown of Nazareth to Bethlehem; there is no room for them at the inn and so Mary gives birth to her firstborn son in a stable and places him in a feeding trough for animals; with great rejoicing, an angel of the Lord appears to nearby shepherds informing them that a Savior has been born, who is Christ the Lord; they go and find Mary and Joseph and the baby in the manger, just as the angel had said. The shepherds leave, glorifying God, while Mary ponders the whole event in her heart. Eight days later, when the child is circumcised, Mary and Joseph give him the name Jesus.

Rahner begins his reflection on this familiar story by noting how Jesus "subjects himself to time." The Word of God "risked entering into this dull reality to become a troublesome outcast, the member of a dispossessed family, and a citizen of an enslaved land." His birth on the outskirts is unrecognized, hardly suitable for the arrival of God on our earth. Jesus came into the world as have all of us, subject to the human condition, on a journey that includes joys and sorrows, and culminates in death. Christian faith sees, in this time-bound story, the appearance of God in human history. Through the birth of Jesus, God's love for human beings appears in a definitive way. Only this core Christian conviction makes human existence, with all its senseless suffering, bearable. Christ, born as a member of our race, is God's final word spoken to the world, establishing the inevitable victory of divine grace over all the darkness of life. Thus it is fitting that the angels rejoice at the birth of Jesus. Rahner concludes by inviting further reflection on the Word made flesh who is "the source both of our disturbing restlessness and of our heartfelt joy."

The Private Life of Jesus[14]

It is important to reflect on the private life of Jesus, even though we know so little about it. The Evangelist Luke tells us that Jesus grew in wisdom, age, and grace, suggesting that he experienced normal human development. He lived a very normal life in Nazareth, the difficult life of a Galilean peasant under the control of the Roman occupying power and its unjust tax system. His religious sensibilities were shaped by the regular practice of his Jewish heritage, including daily prayer, immersion in the Scriptures, and periodic celebrations of the great feasts. He earned a living doing manual labor as a carpenter. Jesus did all this without attracting any special notice from his neighbors in Nazareth, suggesting that he must have adapted to his life situation spontaneously and naturally. Moreover, it seems remarkable that Jesus waited so long to begin his public ministry, especially since we can presume he was anxious to undertake his life mission.

We can imagine Jesus practicing the virtue of patience as he spent a big part of his life waiting. As Rahner points out, for most of us patient waiting is a difficult, challenging task. Our patience is tested on a daily basis by normal interruptions and delays that come our way. In a broader perspective, each phase of our life has its own importance but must eventually give way to the next phase as we constantly move into an unknown future. It is often difficult to determine if we have moved into the next phase of life too soon or waited too long, but our Christian faith calls us to accept the harsh truth that we cannot control future developments and must wait patiently for what we cannot plan. In developing the virtue of patient waiting, Jesus, who waited so long to start his public mission, remains our model.

Jesus Remains in the Temple[15]

At the age of twelve, Jesus makes a pilgrimage with his parents to Jerusalem to worship Yahweh in fulfillment of the law. Respect for the Jewish law characterized the whole life of Jesus. He said he came not to abolish the law but to fulfill it. At the very end of his life, Jesus was still living out his Jewish heritage as he celebrated a Passover meal with his disciples. Rahner says Jesus lived "in the flesh of religion." His humility allowed Jesus, "the most spiritual person to submit himself to forms and laws coming from without." Furthermore, Jesus formed a community of disciples who carried on the ritual practices of baptism and Eucharist and established institutional forms. As Christians today, our spiritual lives are "regulated by laws and precepts." For Rahner, as long as we journey in darkness "the highest type of religious experiences and the most intense love must be governed by certain external laws." To put that religious truth in context, Rahner reminds us that Jesus also taught us to worship in spirit and truth, conscious that God always remains greater than all external signs and institutional forms.

Rahner also invites us to ponder the conflictual aspect of the story. Jesus remains behind in the temple without telling his father and mother. This causes them great distress and anxiety. He chooses to follow the sovereign call of God, even though this means violating the fourth commandment that mandated honor be given to parents. The tension between Jesus and his parents is real, but it is not caused by sin or malice on either side. In making application to us, Rahner notes the common human tendency to assume that the conflicts we experience in life are due to some sort of malice such as pride or narrow-mindedness, usually assigned to the other individuals or groups. This assumption, often wrong, can only poison conflicts and delay their resolution. Conflicts occur inevitably in various settings: family relationships, neighborhood interactions, political debates, culture wars, and international interactions. Rahner highlights some common ecclesial conflicts: between clergy and laity, between contemporary life and canon law, and between "the movement of the Spirit and written regulations." We have a better chance of dealing with these tensions constructively if we assume good will on both sides. The story of the conflict between Jesus and his parents suggests that tensions in life can be transformed into positive energy if we accept them with humility and love.

Rahner goes on to suggest we think of the temple event as a coming of age story in which Jesus learns to become more responsive to the Spirit in following his Father's will. Rahner imagines that Jesus knows "a tormenting loneliness" in the temple and a deep emotional pain in hurting his parents, without being able to offer a satisfactory explanation. Jesus was exercising the "charismatic element" in his life, a responsiveness to the Spirit that goes outside of traditional norms, customs, and laws. He responded to God's will without consulting his parents or getting their permission. Rahner applies this to the Christian life, which is always more than just following traditional forms. There is a proper existential ethics that bids us to follow the promptings of the Spirit who addresses us by name in all our particularity. We need a charismatic element in the church, so that the faith community can gradually discover its full potential for effective witness to Christ. As Rahner strikingly puts it: "God has not resigned in favor of the Church's administrative apparatus." With his typical balance, he goes on to insist that charismatic gifts make their biggest impact by remaining in the church, where they can be supported and guided by its official machinery. The first pilgrimage of Jesus to the temple is a surprisingly rich resource for reflecting on our spiritual quest: the potential value of institutional forms for guiding our journey; healthy ways of dealing with the inevitable conflicts of life; and the importance of listening for the unique call of God within an ecclesial context.

Wedding Feast of Cana [16]

In John's gospel, Jesus works the first of his seven great signs at the wedding feast in Cana of Galilee. Rahner imagines the joyful scene: "people are drinking and laughing" and "the wine is good." Everyone is contributing to the joyful mood, including Jesus who "fits into the context" and is in no way a killjoy. On the contrary, he "loves human beings" and "their earth and their joys, the flavor of wine and the carefree laughter from childlike hearts." Rahner adds: "Later on, people who cannot stand themselves will even call him a carouser and a drunk." At Cana, Jesus works his first miracle, "quietly and unobtrusively," so that the joyful celebration can continue. He came into this world "to redeem the flesh," to teach people "to believe they can be human beings for all eternity without becoming either animals or angels." Inspired by Christ, we "can love the earth and God" because the earth is "the sacrament of God" and God is the creator and fulfillment of the earth. The miracle of Cana brought a brief moment of joyful celebration for the wedding guests, but it continues to speak to us of our brother Jesus who loved this earth and redeemed it for all eternity.

Jesus Tempted in the Desert [17]

Before Jesus begins his public ministry, he goes to the desert to fast and pray. In preparation for preaching the reign of God, he seeks union with his Father in heaven. By withdrawing to the desert, he leaves behind everything needed for human survival in order to seek God, undistracted by any finite reality. Through this action, Jesus proclaims to all of us an essential truth of life, which Rahner expresses this way: "one thing only is necessary, that I be with God, that I find God." Everything else is secondary and must be sacrificed for love of God.

Continuing his meditation, Rahner notes the common element in the three temptations of Jesus: the discrepancy between what he knew about himself as the Son of God and his experience of hunger, neglect, and weakness in the desert. In each temptation, Satan urges Jesus to use his power to avoid suffering, but Jesus refuses to opt out of the human condition and resigns himself to the poverty, loneliness, and limitation shared by all humans. As Rahner points out, this self-emptying of Jesus enables us to identify with him and to learn from his example that acceptance of life on its own terms is an essential component of Christian spiritualty.

Jesus Multiplies the Loaves[18]

The story of the feeding of the multitude is found six times in the gospels, the most attested of the miracles of Jesus. The story line is familiar: the disciples suggest Jesus dismiss the crowd because it is late and they have no food. Jesus tells them to feed the people themselves. They don't have enough, so Jesus blesses the loaves and fishes, and all have enough to eat with a large amount left over. In commenting on the story, Rahner identifies Jesus as a prophet who speaks the Word of God and as a compassionate man who attends to the physical needs of people. Teaching in a deserted place, Jesus draws a large crowd, hungering to hear the word of God. While delivering words of eternal life, Jesus becomes aware that they are getting hungry, and with typical compassion, he satisfies their physical hunger. The people respond by wanting to make Jesus their king so that they can have a continuing source of material goods. At that point Jesus withdraws from the crowd, returning to the mountain.

Rahner sees the story as a commentary on the common human temptation to want more, despite already having enough. He thinks this tendency is intensified in our technological age, which makes so many goods readily available. We can see this as a form of consumerism that puts emphasis on achieving happiness by acquiring more and more things. Our Christian challenge is to keep our priorities straight. Following Christ's teaching is more important than acquiring additional material goods. Concluding on a positive note, Rahner points out that the things of this world have a fundamental goodness. Used properly, they can bring us closer to Christ.

The Transfiguration[19]

Rahner begins his meditation on the transfiguration of Jesus by reminding us that Jesus "had a human heart susceptible to joy and sorrow, pain and consolation." There was "a place in his soul" for "changes of joy and sadness, jubilation and lamentation." Jesus wept and knew moments of happiness. He was "filled with joy, with zest, stirred by compassion, shaken unto death and deceived." He was like us in all things but sin.

During his public ministry, Jesus had to endure a great deal of misunderstanding, opposition, and rejection. In Galilee, the early enthusiasm soon dissipated as people "sought miracles and bread more than faith." Both Pharisees and Sadducees opposed him. In Jerusalem the religious establishment saw him as a threat to their authority and position. His disciples had great trouble understanding the deeper meaning of his teaching, and his people rejected his claim to messiahship. There still remains for him "only one thing: suffering and the cross."

Rahner imagines an emotionally distressed Jesus getting Peter, James, and John to accompany him up Mount Tabor for an evening of prayer away from the busy noise of the world. Jesus treasured his times of prayer to his heavenly Father. Now on the mountain, his intense union with God "fills up all the chambers of his soul, it embraces his body, drawing it, too, into the blessedness of God's light and God's unity." The face of Jesus was like the sun, and his clothes were radiant as light.

The presence of Moses and Elijah is a sign that Jesus is the fulfillment of the Law and "the wellspring" of the Spirit at work in all the prophets. Jesus talks with them about his impending death, which will release the Spirit for the redemption of all people. As at his baptism, the voice of his Father confirms that "this poor, praying Jesus, consecrated for suffering, and heroically prepared for the cross, is God's very beloved Son." Rahner concludes that in the transfiguration, the heart of Jesus finds in God "power which turns a dying into a victory and into the redemption of the world."

Jesus Casting Out Demons[20]

The gospels present Jesus as an exorcist who cured people by casting out demons. In Luke 11:14-23, he drove out a demon from a man who was mute, and the man began to speak and the crowds were amazed. Some claimed that he exorcised people by the power of Beelzebul, the prince of demons. Jesus argued that this did not make logical sense, and that he actually drove out demons by the finger of God, indicating that the kingdom of God is present. Commenting on the exorcism, Rahner says it suggests the fundamental outlook of Jesus on all finite worldly realities: everything created by God has a fundamental goodness; but, at the same time, everything finite is threatened by demonic forces.

Giving this gospel passage a social dimension beyond its original intent, Rahner says it contains an implication that "every Christian has a cultural mission" to challenge demonic powers and to spread the kingdom of God. Christians are called not simply to pray that the kingdom comes but to participate actively in the humanizing of culture. The earthly culture is not the kingdom but is "a kind of sacramental sign" that God loves the world despite its sinfulness and "enfolds it in the love of his creative will." The eyes of faith see all that is "sound, pure, true and mature" in our world as a grace of Christ. Christians have the mission to name that grace and to extend and intensify its impact.

By the same token, Christians are also called to name the demonic elements in the culture and to enter the battle against them. Rahner warns against deceiving ourselves in this matter. It is easy to overlook evil tendencies because they are widespread and everyone accepts them. Conscious that we have not directly contributed to these cultural evils, we may find ourselves "drifting with the tide accepting as self-evident a culture that has been made diabolical by the forces of debasement."

Furthermore, it is difficult for Christians who become aware of cultural evil to know how to respond. There is the danger of trying to impose the "old values" on today's world, thus "merely preserving what was evil yesterday" in the fight against what is evil today. On the other hand, "we cannot fulfill our cultural mission by just saying yes and amen to every current trend." A contemporary Christian spirituality calls for a discernment of spirits, prudent judgments, and courage to work for a "Christian, purified and exorcised culture." This is, of course, a mission that will find its completion only at the end time. "Christian leaven, when mixed with the dough of this world, is fated never to become entirely pure, entirely radiant, entirely aflame." Still we must labor on, alert to signs of the presence of the kingdom and always reliant on the power of Christ, the exorcist who cast out demons and assured the final victory over them.

Rahner's interpretation of the exorcising activity of Jesus has kinship with important themes of liberation theology, such as social sin, systemic evil, false consciousness, orthopraxis, and the liberating power of Christ. Rahner himself said he did not fully understand liberation theology, but he supported the liberation theologians, including Gustavo Gutierrez, and enunciated themes supportive of the liberational movement. His reflection on Christ the exorcist makes that clear.

Jesus Teaching[21]

In chapter 8 of John's gospel, Jesus is teaching in the treasury in the temple area. He presents himself as the Light of the World that overcomes the darkness, as the Ambassador of the Father, and as One greater than Abraham. Rahner uses John's portrayal of the superiority of Jesus over Abraham as a basis for discussing the way Jesus understood himself. Rahner does not distinguish John's Christology from the self-perception of the historical Jesus. In other words, he is basing his meditation on the distinct understanding of Jesus found in John's gospel. With that in mind, let us consider Rahner's four main points.

First, the Johannine Jesus, expressing his human thoughts, says, "before Abraham was, I am." Jesus knows he is the one who "dwells with the Father from all eternity." He "feels it in his bones," as Rahner phrases it, that he is God present in the world. Second, Jesus views himself as one who not only speaks the truth but is the truth. He is "at one with himself"; he knows who he is and what he wants; and he understands himself perfectly. His soul is not "brittle, fragmentary, obscure, discordant and opaque," but strong, whole, clear, and harmonious. Third, Jesus does not seek his own glory but does the will of his Father. He embodies "selflessness, defenselessness, service, devotion, self-effacement," and sheer mercy. He is the "true middle, the mediator who unites us with the Father." Finally, Jesus knows that he is "the sinless one," a conviction he holds in "the infinite humility of his human heart," without boasting or self-assertion. After recounting all of these marvelous qualities of Jesus, Rahner insists that they need not separate us from him. We too are God's children, born of divine love. We also share in God's truth by participating in the life of Christ. We are touched by divine love, as was Jesus. The Spirit empowers us, as it did Jesus, to do the will of God and spread the kingdom in the world. Christ, the model of fulfilled humanity, helps us know ourselves better as sons and daughters of God and to appreciate the way grace is at work in our lives.

The Last Supper[22]

On the night before he died, Jesus sat together with those he called friends for a final meal. He sat with them at table, as he often had, because the common sharing of bread and wine expresses the fellowship of fidelity and love. He sat with them for one last time because he knew he had to go alone to the "outermost darkness and solitude of death," as Rahner phrases it. During the meal, he shares with them bread and wine, which "through the power of his creative word," have become his body and blood. In that sharing, the disciples are united to Christ and "embraced by love which joins them to each other." The sacred meal anticipates the eternal banquet when Christ will complete his redemptive work.

Looking for a way to express the "unfathomable mystery" of this farewell meal, Rahner employs evocative language. "In that hour Jesus accepted his death as the giving of himself to God for the redemption of the world." Jesus "bravely walks" toward his death, "a life-bearing death," that touches "the innermost being" of the disciples who through their table fellowship with Christ are "encircled by the grace of God."

At the end of the meal, Jesus tells his disciples: "Do this in remembrance of me." Faithful to this command, the church celebrates the eucharistic meal, which makes present for us the new and eternal covenant established by Christ. He is for us "the crucified One and the resurrected One," "the eternal grounds" for trusting ourselves to God, "the lover" who experienced "the deepest helplessness of being human" so completely that it "became victory itself." When we celebrate in remembrance of the Last Supper, we proclaim the abiding presence of Christ "as pledge of eternal life," as "the beginning of the transformation of the world," and as "the irresistible presence of the glory of God in the darkness of sin."

By celebrating the Eucharist, "we ourselves are contained in the yes of the Son to the unfathomable ordinance of the Father." We join with Christ in offering praise and thanks to God. In the power of the Eucharist, as the presence of Christ's love, "everything becomes recommitted, everything opens up, everything finds its solution." Rahner concludes his reflection on the Last Supper with a reminder that all the meaning and power of the Eucharist becomes operative in us in proportion to our faith and our openness to God's grace.

The Agony in the Garden[23]

Following his usual custom, Jesus goes to the garden of Gethsemane after the Last Supper, aware that Judas the betrayer will look for him there. He takes with him the disciples of Tabor who experienced the transfiguration, but they deal with their anxiety by falling asleep. In his moment of need, Jesus is left with companions who do not understand him and have no consolation to offer. In his commentary, Rahner notes that Jesus accepts his Father's will and therefore, "lets his strength trickle out in weakness, his courage drown in fear and his love sink into the darkness of Godforsakenness." He is "immersed in deadly anxiety" and "overpowered by something he apparently cannot control." His cry for help is "drowned in silence." The Father "leaves His Son crushed, covered with bloody sweat, powerless." And yet out of that "mute nothingness, into which the agony of his cry disappears, comes something wonderful" as Jesus receives the energy to rise up and accept his cross.

Rahner interprets the whole agony in the garden in terms of strength encountering weakness. Jesus, the Son of God, "falls on his face" and loses all power. He is confronted with the absolute futility of his work. He had given himself totally to establishing the reign of God, and now he has to face the failure of his mission. Jesus asks that he be spared the chalice of failure and suffering that is "sheer horror" and "absolute impotence." Despite this agony, Jesus accepts the chalice, commits once again to doing God's will and in the process transforms the cup of suffering into the new and eternal covenant. Applying the example of Jesus to our own "Gethsemane-existence," Rahner repeats the good news: "there is no darkness in which God does not live," and "no abyss greater than the abyss of divine love and mercy." Jesus, who suffered such emotional torment in the garden, remains for us a sign of hope, especially when we meet defeat and failure on the spiritual journey. The darkest moments cannot finally prevail over the light of divine love.

Betrayal[24]

Judas, the betrayer, came to the garden with temple police to arrest Jesus. The disciples fled, including Peter, who said he was ready to die with his master. Jesus is "thrust into the terrible loneliness of the man who is abandoned, betrayed, rejected."

Rahner invites meditation on the "Godlessness of sin," manifested in the betrayal by Judas. Sin is the rejection of divine love and a "fundamental perversion of loyalty." It is "a degradation of the creatures' relationship to God" and "a darkening of one's own mind." Nevertheless, wherever sin exists, grace abounds all the more, as the apostle Paul teaches us. Rahner specifies this Christian confidence: "God's faithfulness remains even in betrayal, and, in fact, achieves its end through it." For Christian spirituality, Judas remains a striking reminder of the abiding threat of sin, while Jesus, the apparent victim, represents the transforming power of divine grace.

Jesus before the Sanhedrin[25]

Roughly treated, Jesus is dragged before the Sanhedrin, accused of blasphemy worthy of death. He is condemned in the name of good order, national pride, the good of the country, and belief in Yahweh. The religious authorities do not accept the sworn testimony of Jesus that he is the long-awaited Messiah. Rahner points out that the "Sanhedrin mentality" remains alive today, even in the church, when people "presuppose a certain power over God," or criticize God "in the name of one's own limited knowledge," or confine God's immense love to "our limited measuring rods." Paradoxically, through his condemnation by the Sanhedrin, our Lord calls us to open our hearts to the liberating love of God that challenges all religious small-mindedness.

Jesus before Pilate[26]

Before Pilate, who represents the vast power of the Roman Empire, Jesus stands in noble silence. To the pagans, the preaching of Jesus is foolishness. Pilate is so worried about the disputes surrounding Jesus that he is prepared to let an innocent man be executed for the sake of peace and order. The governor is guided by a worldly wisdom that may seem clever but is really a superficial reading of the situation. Rahner asks us to see if Pilate's sense of worldly wisdom has invaded our own consciousness and influenced our behavior. A genuine Christian spirituality does not settle for a cool, rational, worldly wisdom but strives for the kind of noble simplicity and dedication to truth manifested by Jesus before the Roman governor.

Jesus Tortured[27]

Pilate released Barabbas, but Jesus he scourged and delivered to be crucified. The gospels do not go into detail, but this is a direct attack on the Lord's body. Rahner sees it as "a sadistic attack made by a callous soldier," which amounted to a violation of the personhood of Jesus inflicted by "human malice and depravity." After the scourging Pilate says: "Behold the man." Rahner invites us to behold this disfigured man and perceive the face of God. Jesus is carrying in his body the sinfulness of the world and the personal wickedness of human beings who are always ready to justify their vile deeds. But he bears these marks of sin in order to transform them into signs of God's compassionate care. By following Jesus, we can achieve "a true humanism" that has no illusions about human existence but can face all the dark forces with confidence in the power of divine grace. This Son of Man mocked and tortured is truly "the Glorified One," the "One who carried his passion into glory."

The Death of Jesus on the Cross[28]

The cruel death of Jesus on the cross is both the high point of his mission and the supreme catastrophe of his life. Jesus is betrayed, abandoned by his friends, and rejected by the religious leaders of his people. He feels abandoned by his Father and "his mission seems to disappear into deadly silence." At the same time, his death is "the deepest and most personal act of his life." It is the hour of his glorification, the reason he came into the world. All of his life Jesus was obedient to the will of his Father. This submissive obedience to God has, as Rahner puts it, a "certain mystical sense" about it that defies our usual categories. By his obedience, Jesus absorbs "that which is totally foreign to him, the sinfulness of the world," and transforms it into the power of God's love. The obedience of Jesus is "the silent Yes" to his excruciating death, intensified by his sense of abandonment.

According to Rahner, the death of Jesus was not only an act of acceptance of suffering but also a loving "Yes" to "the incomprehensibility of God." It is only through love that human beings can express their essence and escape the prison of selfishness. Throughout his life, Jesus endured the ultimately mysterious character of God, and this act of loving endurance reached its climax on the cross, expressed in his cry "My God, my God, why have you abandoned me." It was this same self-emptying love that prompted Jesus to promise a thief crucified with him the gift of paradise. A lifetime of following God's will prepared Jesus to declare with ultimate trust: "Father, into your hands I commend my spirit." The incarnate Word who knew "the dignity of a mission, the abyss of ruin, the consummation of obedience and the deep love of the heart" surrendered himself into his Father's hands.

As followers of Jesus, we are called to take up the cross. This is a most difficult challenge, and we all know the temptation to escape the cross, perhaps in subtle and disguised ways. Moreover, Rahner reminds us that human existence "offers an abundance of suffering and futility which cannot be mastered by sober courage alone." Given a sense of our own limitations, we turn to the crucified Lord to provide the strength we need to manage this suffering without falling into despair, cynicism, and a sterile resignation. Our Christian calling is "to continue the sacrifice of the Lord in our own lives," trusting that this leads to eternal life.

The Risen Christ[29]

The gospels give witness to the resurrection of Jesus through reports of the empty tomb and, more importantly, various appearances to his disciples, including Mary of Magdala, Thomas the Twin, Peter and the other apostles, and Cleopas and his companion. These stories do not comprise a consistent narrative and cannot be harmonized. We cannot determine if Jesus first appeared in Jerusalem or Galilee, nor whether he appeared first to Mary of Magdala or Peter. In these stories, Jesus is typically not immediately recognized; for example Mary at first takes him for the gardener. Rahner believes that these appearances are "secondary clarifications of an appearance of the risen Jesus which properly lies behind these visions." The early witnesses were all convinced that Jesus lives on and that his cause "was not invalidated by his death." We do not need "to visualize to ourselves the peculiar nature of his physical risen existence," especially since we cannot really imagine the glorified life of Christ, which is outside our time-space framework. Our faith is not finally based on a report of the empty tomb or objective eyewitness accounts of the first disciples. Rather, we hear the appearance accounts as statements of faith in the context of our own experiences—simple and ordinary as they might be—of the power of the risen Lord. We can, for example, relate the story of Thomas to situations when the risen Christ has strengthened us to say "My Lord and my God" in the midst of nagging doubts. We can compare the Emmaus story to the times we have recognized Christ in the eucharistic liturgy. All the New Testament appearance stories interact with our specific experience of the risen Christ to form, as Rahner phrases it, "one testimony" that Jesus lives.

In leading our meditation on the risen Christ, Rahner wants us to keep in mind that the death and resurrection and exaltation of Jesus form one unified event, the paschal mystery. Christian life is always sustained and guided by that paschal mystery. We follow the crucified and risen One. We cannot celebrate Easter without Good Friday, which remains an ignominious failure without the resurrection. Distortions in spirituality are inevitable when the paschal dialectic collapses: for example, without the cross, piety seeks cheap grace and utopian dreams; and without Easter, life becomes pointless and suffering has no redeeming value.

Jesus is raised to life as a whole person. As Rahner insists, divine love seized "the totality of his concrete human existence—including his body." His whole destiny and everything he experienced on earth has "entered into the glory of the Father." When raised by his Father, Jesus left nothing behind; not his cross, not his abandonment, not his death. He remains for us the crucified and risen Lord.

For Rahner, the resurrection is the firm foundation for hope in a world that knows so much suffering. Contemplating the risen Christ, eyes of faith recognize that the seeds of the final victory of good over evil have been planted. In his death, Jesus plunged into the heart of the world, a mixture of grace and sin at the deepest level; through his resurrection he has not abandoned the world but redeemed it at its very roots. Now a positive outcome of human history is assured. Death has lost its ultimate power over human beings. Love will be tested but never totally defeated. Christians have no recipe for ridding the world of sin. Sin remains an abiding factor in human existence; death and futility continue to stalk the earth. Christian spirituality, however, does foster a calm realization or "courage for victory" that we can face the evil in the world because Christ has conquered all the demonic forces and assured the triumph of God's blessings.

The Ascension of Jesus[30]

The Acts of the Apostles has the most explicit and vivid report of the ascension of Jesus. After his death and resurrection, Christ appeared to his disciples over a forty-day period instructing them about the reign of God. He tells them not to depart from Jerusalem but to wait for the promised Spirit. Empowered by this Spirit, the disciples will give witness to Christ to the ends of the earth. With that, he was lifted up and a cloud took him from their sight. Rahner recognizes that modern science does not allow us to take this description of Jesus going up in the heavens literally, but he insists that this scientific advance is a proper Christian development that prompts us to reinterpret the ascension and its meaning for today. In the context of the old cosmology, Christians could think of heaven as a place existing before the time of Christ, who opened its gates through his death and resurrection. In the context of modern cosmology, Rahner suggests that we think of the ascension as establishing heaven and recognize Christ as "the founder of heaven." This enables us to speak of heaven in terms of human fulfillment rather than as a place where disembodied souls go after death.

For Rahner, the feast of the Ascension is a celebration of Christ's presence, not his absence. True, he has left this earth, which was his physical home for over three decades. During that time he was confined to a tiny space and a brief period. Through his death and exaltation he is now present to all people in all places and times. As promised, Christ is now present through his Spirit who dwells within us. We carry this Spirit with us wherever we go as an inexhaustible source of energy and guidance. From this perspective, we can better appreciate the statement of Jesus that we are better off if he departs. Rahner adds that the ascension, "the universal event of salvation history," is especially helpful when "the lights of the world grow dark" and we experience "an emptiness of the heart." Then the Ascension, a feast of abiding presence, strikes us as especially good news.

Individually, these profound and insightful meditations of Rahner help us to see Jesus with fresh eyes and suggest specific ways of following his good example. Collectively, they demonstrate the concrete Christocentric character of Rahner's theology as well as its spiritual and pastoral relevance.

Church:
Renewing Ecclesial Life

Rahner's ecclesiology, the study of the church, flows organically from his Christology.[1] The church is the sacrament of the risen Lord, the community that keeps alive the memory of Jesus, the institution that carries on his mission of spreading the reign of God in the world. The church fosters the Christian life by worshiping God through the sacraments, especially the Eucharist, and by practicing love of neighbor in the world, especially attending to those in need. Far from being a merely speculative study of the church, Rahner's ecclesiology is filled with practical suggestions for spiritual growth and pastoral ministry. This becomes more apparent when we examine four specific challenges the church faces in today's world: the divorce of spirituality from religion; the mass exodus of Catholics from the church; the proper interpretation of Vatican II; and the renewal of parish life.

Spiritual but Not Religious

Today, many good people, especially among the millennial generation, say they are spiritual but not religious. This is a contemporary version of a previous movement that said "yes" to Jesus but "no" to the church. In response, Rahner insists that Christianity is necessarily ecclesial because God's grace, which touches all dimensions of life, seeks visibility.[2] The divine self-communication calls for a free personal response that has an external public dimension. This is true because human beings are enfleshed spirits, interdependent social beings who come to fulfillment in community life. Rahner thought that a rugged individualism was outmoded for people today serious about spiritual growth. A full Christian life involves participation in the church because Christ's message is authoritative and confronts us as an objective reality and because we work out our salvation not in private isolation but in real life, which always has a communal and institutional dimension. Rahner recognized that some people are religiously tone deaf, with little appreciation of the rituals, creeds, and doctrines that constitute organized religion. These individuals may still be holy people and should not be treated as spiritually inferior. At the same time, the pastoral task is to connect spirituality and religion, to demonstrate that religious doctrines and practices are designed to express and stir up the spiritual dimension of human existence. Doctrines are not merely statements of belief but have the important function of highlighting specific ways that God touches human existence and of encouraging a positive response to these divine gifts. Rituals, always in danger of formalism and magical interpretations, are meant to stretch the imagination, to lift the soul to God in worship, and to form community with fellow searchers. Making this case in the contemporary world is a difficult task but well worthwhile, so that more people can say "I am spiritual and therefore I am religious."

The Exodus of Catholics

The numbers are indeed alarming. According to a 2008 survey by the Pew Forum on Religion and Public Life, one out of every three adult Americans who were raised Catholic have left the church. There are about 22 million former Catholics in the United States, slightly over 10 percent of the adult population. If they were regarded as a distinct denomination, they would be the second largest Christian body in the country.

About half of former Catholics joined Protestant denominations, while the other half are no longer affiliated with any church. The unaffiliated are a diverse group, including explicit atheists, committed secular humanists, and those who have drifted away and feel no need for institutional religion. According to the Pew survey, many of the unaffiliated do have disagreements with church teaching on issues such as the role of women, homosexuality, abortion, divorce and remarriage, birth control, and clerical celibacy. Placed in a larger context, these former Catholics are part of the growing number of Americans of various backgrounds who claim no religious affiliation. Some sociologists argue that this recent development in the United States is the delayed result of the modern secularization process that has already eroded religious affiliation in Europe and will eventually cause the demise of religion among most enlightened people.

Scholars have pointed out that our current situation is still influenced by various modern developments: the Enlightenment conviction that reason is the key to human progress; the Romantic ideal of human flourishing in all dimensions of life; the success of political democracy with its separation of church and state; the growth of free market economies; and the reform movements that have sought to improve society by rational planning. These and other modern movements do create a context where ordinary people can choose to live without religious beliefs and rituals. Thus a growing number of people today seek the good life without any apparent need for religion. They may well be productive citizens, good family members, industrious workers, and helpful friends without any explicit relationship to a religious tradition. Clearly, we face a great pastoral challenge as large numbers leave the church, including people of good will who function well without the support of institutional religion.

Fifty years ago in his book *The Christian Commitment*, Rahner predicted this decline in the number of church members in developed countries and offered some perspectives on this inevitable trend. In an ideal world, we could imagine all people becoming members of the church in fulfillment of God's will. In reality, however, the modern church will remain a "diaspora community," a minority living in an increasingly pluralistic world. The secularization process that grants autonomy to politics, economics, and other areas of common life is actually in accord with the impulse of the Gospel. Christianity does not demand that the church have control over the social order. Believers do not have a complete blueprint for how to organize society. The medieval Christendom that placed all areas of life under the authority of the church was the result of historical factors, and not a necessary embodiment of Christian faith. Rahner claims that the diaspora situation of the church is a "must," which means that it is the inevitable consequence of fidelity to the thrust of the Gospel. Moreover, elements of Christian faith will remain operative in secular movements.

Given the ready availability of various worldviews, the church will inevitably lose members. Rahner advises us to avoid the "tyranny of numbers" and to accept the numerical loses with trust in God and a calm spirit. He quotes Augustine: "Many whom God has, the Church does not have." Individuals who live out an exclusive humanism may well be on good terms with their Creator and Judge. Parents who have sons and daughters who no longer practice the faith may be understandably disappointed, but they can trust that the merciful God holds their children in gracious hands. Eyes sensitive to hidden grace may detect Gospel values still operative in the lives of former church members.

Christian Humanism

Paradoxically, Rahner contends that a calm acceptance of these unavoidable losses frees us for an aggressive, self-confident effort to persuade people to maintain or initiate church membership. A key element in this effort is to articulate and exemplify a Christian humanism that promotes personal growth and works for justice and peace in the world. We are stamped with the divine image, graced with the Holy Spirit, blessed with an inherent dignity and worth. God calls us to develop our talents and actualize our potential in order to serve the common good. Jesus Christ exemplifies human existence at its best, reminding us of what we are called to be. Furthermore, he shares with us the mission to make the world a better place. For Christians, love of God and love of neighbor are essentially and inextricably related. Prayer and worship reflect and fuel the struggle to create a more just, verdant, and peaceful world. Christian humanism embraces many values and goals of secular humanism but enhances them by providing a context of ultimate meaning, the energy of spiritual motivation, and protection against restrictive ideologies. The claims of a faith-based humanism gain persuasive power when committed Christians live it out on a daily basis and draw on it to guide their participation in the political, economic, and social realms of life.

Rahner insists that modern pluralism can actually strengthen the church despite the unavoidable loss of members. More people will be churchgoing believers because they have made a conscious choice and not just because they were born Catholic. Increasingly, individuals will maintain their Christian belief because they have experienced the power of Christ and his Gospel in some concrete way and not merely out of habit or custom. A church with fewer but more committed members has a better chance of being a genuine sign of the risen Christ and an effective instrument of his mission in the world. Furthermore, a church that celebrates and exemplifies Christian humanism is more likely to attract new members who come to recognize that a transcendent humanism is more robust and attractive than a self-contained secular humanism.

A pastorally sensitive approach to the exodus from the Catholic Church would have to examine the distinctive motives of those who join mainline Protestant churches, as well as those who affiliate with Evangelical congregations. It would also have to make a more nuanced analysis of the unaffiliated, and propose a broad range of pastoral responses. In addressing all these concerns, however, it seems wise to keep Rahner's advice in mind: trust God and avoid the tyranny of numbers, while working calmly but wholeheartedly to make the church a more credible and attractive sign of Christ's humanizing message for the world.

Interpreting Vatican II

A third challenge facing the contemporary church is how to interpret the teachings of the Second Vatican Council. Fifty years after Pope John XXIII opened the council on October 11, 1962, the church is still in the process of appropriating and fulfilling the dominant vision that informs its major documents. These texts reflect traditional teaching as well as the modern renewal movements in Scripture, liturgy, ecumenism, and theology. As a result, the church moved in directions now familiar to us: more active participation in the liturgy; greater appreciation of the Scriptures; more emphasis on the role of the laity and the universal call to holiness; greater openness to ecumenical and interfaith dialogue; a deeper sense of responsibility for humanizing culture and transforming society; and a stronger commitment to the proposition that we are the church.

From the viewpoint of these striking developments, Vatican II appears as the culmination of the various reform movements that gathered momentum throughout the twentieth century and achieved official recognition in the conciliar documents. Within that framework, scholars continue to debate whether major conciliar teachings on important issues, like liturgy, religious liberty, ecumenism, world religions, and the church in the world, are in continuity with the previous Catholic teachings or diverge from them in significant ways. At the popular level, this debate divides Catholics who favor the progressive spirit of reform initiated by the council and those who are more attuned to traditional expressions of the faith. To keep this division in proper perspective, we should remember that younger Catholics have no direct memory of Vatican II and are not really concerned about how to interpret its teachings.

World Church

About five years before his death in 1984, Rahner gave a lecture in the United States on the "Basic Theological Interpretation of the Second Vatican Council" later published in *Theological Investigations,* which suggested a radically different way of interpreting the council.[3] Without totally rejecting the culmination explanation, Rahner invites us to view the council as the rudimentary beginning of a new era in which the church will explicitly understand itself for the first time as a world church and will function accordingly. A fully realized world church will not be dominated by European and American bishops and will not function like an "export firm" that disseminates a Roman version of Christianity around the world. It will understand itself as a communion of various local churches all rooted in their native cultures. In the world church, indigenous expressions of Christianity will interact with one another to enrich the universal church.

Rahner, who was an official expert at Vatican II, admits that the council recognized this new self-understanding only in an unformed and tentative fashion. Under the guidance of the Holy Spirit, the bishops produced documents with implications greater than they could realize. In retrospect, we can detect intimations of an emerging world church in the work of the council. In contrast to the First Vatican Council in 1870, native bishops from various countries in

Asia and Africa were active participants in Vatican II. They gathered with their European and American colleagues not as an advisory board to the pope but as a collegial body, with and under the bishop of Rome, exercising supreme teaching authority for the whole church. Although these native bishops were limited in number and influence at the council, they represented the future of a universal church composed of local churches with indigenous hierarchies.

We can also find significant harbingers of the world church in the conciliar documents. The Constitution on the Liturgy made a crucial contribution to a more open church by allowing the use of the vernacular in liturgical celebrations. By expanding the options beyond Latin, the bishops signaled their appreciation of diverse cultures and opened up the possibility of further cultural adaptations of the liturgy. *Gaudium et Spes* (the Pastoral Constitution on the Church in the Modern World) explicitly addressed not only Christians but also the whole human family with all of its joys and sorrows. Although written largely from a European perspective, this groundbreaking document recognized the responsibility of the church to attend to the needs of the larger family of nations, including the developing countries.

In *Nostra Aetate* (the Declaration on the Relation of the Church to Non-Christian Religions), the church, for the first time in its history, officially offered a positive assessment of the world's great religious traditions, declaring its high regard for their doctrines and precepts, which are "rays of that truth which enlightens all people." In a number of places, the bishops expressed optimism about the effectiveness of God's salvific will for all people, restricted only by serious violations of conscience (*Lumen Gentium* 16 and *Gaudium et Spes* 23).

Influenced by the pioneering work of the American theologian John Courtney Murray, *Dignitatis Humanae* (the Declaration on Religious Liberty) recognized the importance of freedom of conscience and renounced the use of coercion or force in preaching the Gospel anywhere in the world. *Unitatis Redintegratio* (the Decree on Ecumenism) encouraged ecumenical dialogue as a means of overcoming the divisions that thwart the worldwide mission of the church. This brief survey suggests that at Vatican II, the church did indeed take initial steps toward thinking and acting like a world church. Taken together, these conciliar teachings can provide a framework for continuing this process under the direction of the Holy Spirit.

SECOND GREAT TRANSITION

In developing his notion of the world church, Rahner suggests that we are now living through the second great transition in the history of the church. The first took place in the first century under the leadership of the apostle Paul, as the primitive community moved from being a predominately Judeo-Christian church to a Gentile church. In this radical shift, Paul did not simply transplant or export the original Jewish understanding of Jesus into the Gentile world. Rather, he took the core of the Christian message, detached from Jewish forms (for example, circumcision, Sabbath observance, dietary laws, and synagogue services), and planted it in the pagan soil of the Roman Empire where it grew over the next two millennia into the European form of Christianity that was still dominant at the Second Vatican Council.

The second great transition in the history of Christianity involves the current ongoing shift from a Western church to a world church. This radical departure, signaled by Vatican II, calls for the church to proclaim the core Christian message, detached from its European and American cultural forms, to native cultures across the globe where it can develop in distinctive ways. A church faithful to its worldwide mission must abandon the failed strategy of exporting Roman Christianity, with its culturally conditioned theology, rituals, and Canon Law, to other parts of the world. With what Rahner calls "Pauline boldness,"[4] the church needs a new form of evangelization that demands both a deeper understanding of the fundamental substance of the Christian message and greater freedom for local cultures to assimilate the core of the faith and creatively express it in appropriate ways. Then the universal church, a communion of communions, will enjoy the fruits of a genuine dialogue between the various cultural expressions of the traditional story of Jesus crucified and risen.

A DIVERSIFIED CHURCH

A truly universal church will be more diversified than the Roman Church we still know fifty years after the council. Dreaming of the possibilities of the world church, Rahner envisions a future pope sitting at a round table in open dialogue with leaders of the world's great religious traditions. In this future church, national conferences of bishops will have greater power to make regional adaptations. Leaders of the Roman Curia will function more as servants than bureaucrats. Liturgical celebrations around the world will more clearly reflect the best of local cultures. Ecumenical and interreligious dialogue will flourish in a genuine search for a truth greater than any group now possesses. Rome will no longer attempt to impose a uniform Canon Law on all local churches. The church will find ways to collaborate with other spiritual traditions in the vital task of creating a more just world.

VATICAN CONTROL

During the pontificates of John Paul II (1978–2006) and Benedict XVI (2006–2013), the Vatican has continued to impose its particular mentality on local churches: for example, overruling the American bishops on a variety of pastoral matters, including the proper time for first sacrament of penance, the use of inclusive language in the Catechism, and the translation of the new Missal mandated for all English-speaking countries. From a Rahnerian perspective, such interventions appear as anachronistic efforts to maintain a system of control that cannot survive long term.

SUPPORT FOR THE WORLD CHURCH

The movement of Vatican II toward the world church finds new energy in important contemporary trends. Demographically, the center of the Christian world has shifted southward away from Europe and North America to Africa, Asia, and Latin America. Given the current trends, by 2025 the largest Christian populations will be in Africa and Latin America, with Asia fourth behind Europe. The growing number of native bishops from the southern hemisphere will surely exert great influence on the universal church as they share their distinctive experiences of living the Christian faith in diverse situations.

The thrust toward a world church envisioned by Rahner also gains momentum from the secular process commonly called "globalization." This movement, fueled by the global economy and shaped by the Internet, has not only deepened our awareness of the essential unity of the human family but has also, paradoxically, produced a new appreciation of the specific riches of particular cultures. A church that believes in the incarnation and reads the signs of the times must match its claims to universality with special attention to the particular needs of various groups around the world. Our global village, where time and space are so compressed, calls for a world church that proclaims the story of Jesus and allows it to develop in dialogue with various cultures.

PASTORAL IMPLICATIONS

Pastorally, Rahner's world church dream functions as a sign of hope for Catholics who favor less Vatican centralization and more autonomy for local churches. For a long time that dream was a distant hope, accompanied by a realistic resignation that it will not happen in the foreseeable future. The election of Pope Francis has already altered that outlook and created a remarkable new mood among many Catholics. His simple lifestyle and genuine care for the poor have touched the hearts of many in the church and outside. His crucial decision to appoint eight cardinals representing diverse geographical regions to help in the governance of the church can be seen as a tiny first step in moving toward a world church. Rahner was convinced that this direction was inevitable, and Catholics now have renewed hope that the initial thrust of Vatican II will enjoy a new springtime of growth.

Renewing Parishes

We can continue to explore the practical import of Rahner's ecclesiology by examining his insights on renewing parish life. With all the attention given to the papacy and large-scale problems like clergy sex abuse, faithful Catholics can sometimes forget the crucial role their local parish plays in their actual experience of the Christian life. We can imagine Catholics who are so upset with the new translation of the Mass prayers that they forget how spiritually nourishing the Sunday liturgies are in their parish. It is possible to let frustration with the hierarchy overshadow the good work done by the parish in serving the poor in the neighborhood.

A Theology of the Parish

Rahner provides a theological perspective that directs our attention to the crucial role of the local parish in manifesting and fostering Christian discipleship. We commonly think of the church as an enduring institution with set creeds, doctrines, rituals, and laws. Rahner, who recognized the need for a more developed theology of the parish, invites us to think of the church as an event. The church is actualized and made real when it acts to worship God and spread the reign of God in the world. This happens most clearly when the community gathers for the eucharistic celebration, which makes the death and resurrection of the Lord present here and now. This is the prime example of the general principle that the church as event must take place at a given time and in a specific place. The church also happens whenever parishioners gather together to participate in Christ's mission to the world: for example, by running a food distribution center for the poor. The parish is not simply a juridical subdivision of the larger church that exists for practical logistical reasons but is, in its essence, an event of the universal church, "the highest degree of actuality of the total Church."[5]

History

Historically, parishes in the United States have played a significant role in the life of Catholic citizens. Catholic immigrants to this country typically settled in urban areas with others of their own nationality. Once settled they acquired land, built churches, and hired priests to serve them. Catholic immigrants, around 3 million by 1880 and over 30 million by 1920, had to deal with the nativist prejudice and an often hostile dominant culture. For them, the parish served as a safe haven, a community that kept alive their ethnic customs, and a center for their spiritual and social lives. During the nineteenth century, laypeople exercised great influence in parish life. They elected lay trustees who ran the parish and had charge of financial matters, including paying the salary of the priest. By 1900, the American bishops gained control over parishes, reserving to themselves ownership of parish property and the appointment of pastors. As a result, the role of laypeople in parish life gradually diminished, leaving them in the passive role commonly known as the "pay, pray and obey syndrome."

World War II

World War II had a great effect on Catholic parishes in the United States. Protestants who served side by side with Catholics in the war found it difficult to maintain the nativist prejudices in all their previous vigor. After the war, Catholics went to college in great numbers through the benefits supplied by the G.I. Bill. This enabled them to get better jobs, make more money, and move into the suburbs where they helped establish new parishes. These parishes functioned more like voluntary associations and less like safe havens from a hostile world. Catholic parishioners, now better educated and socially accepted, expected their priests to provide spiritual nourishment and moral guidance. The suburban parish was no longer the center of parishioners' social lives, but it remained their religious home, and they expected to have input on how it functioned. The election of John Kennedy in 1960, supported by around 80 percent of Catholics, signaled the newfound confidence of many Catholics in their lives as citizens and parishioners.

Vatican II

The Second Vatican Council had an immense effect on parish life in the United States. At Sunday Masses, many parishioners went from silent spectators to full participants, including serving as lectors and eucharistic ministers. Instead of relying on the priest to do all the parish ministry, laypersons took on a great variety of ministerial activities: running religious education programs, serving on parish councils, bringing their expertise to finance councils, preparing couples for marriage, teaching in RCIA programs, taking communion to the sick, preparing families for baptism, and leading parish efforts to assist the needy and promote justice and peace. Priests did less hands-on ministry and spent more time and energy organizing and coordinating the many activities of their parishes.

Parish Life Today

The contrast between parish life before Vatican II and after is striking and instructive. As Rahner has noted, we rediscovered the theology of baptism that calls all the baptized to a life of holiness and service to the church and the world. The growth of lay ecclesial ministry is not simply a pragmatic response to the priest shortage but is rooted in a deeper appreciation of baptism as empowering full engagement in the life of the church. This theology is actualized in local parishes that have implemented the teaching and spirit of Vatican II.

At their best, parishes provide parishioners with opportunities to use their gifts and talents to build up the Body of Christ and spread the kingdom in the world. They celebrate nourishing liturgies with solid homilies that relate the Scriptures to their daily lives, and music that is lively and uplifting. Effective parishes provide religious education programs for adults and children that enable all parishioners to gain a deeper understanding of their faith. They offer a great variety of opportunities for spiritual growth, such as retreats, Bible study, prayer groups, and adoration. Healthy parishes reach out to serve the larger community through Christian service projects and programs to help the needy, as well as through all the efforts of parishioners to humanize the culture and create a more just society and peaceful world. The church as event happens when parishioners gather to worship God and to serve others.

Parish Outreach

In his important book, *The Shape of the Church to Come*, written in 1970 for the German Synod of Bishops, Rahner offers some practical suggestions for improving the local church. A parish should be a community of Christians who have made a free decision to belong and are proactive in trying to Christianize the secular world.[6] To stress the importance of aggressive outreach, Rahner maintained: "It means more to win one new Christian from what we may call neopaganism than to keep ten 'old Christians.'" A parish can attract secularized persons by proclaiming a Christian humanism that celebrates self-actualization and a passion for justice, but in the religious context of an ultimate meaning and a transcendent goal. We can imagine a secular humanist, deeply concerned about poverty in his community, who is attracted to the local church by its compassionate and respectful outreach to the homeless.

Parish Pluralism[7]

A parish should celebrate and model a healthy pluralism among parishioners who have diverse worldviews, theologies, and spiritualities. Although polarization is not the dominant problem in most parishes, parishioners should avoid harsh, unsupported judgments about those who are different. Positively, parishes should foster dialogue and collaboration among diverse groups. Rahner suggests greater interaction among parish groups: for example, the social justice committee could invite members of the respect life movement to its meeting and offer them the opportunity to speak. The point of this strategy is to create personal relationships with those who are different, making it harder to demonize them and easier to collaborate with them in promoting parish harmony and vitality.

A Declericalized Parish[8]

Rahner calls for a church in which pastors realize that the Spirit is at work in all the parishioners and that the charismatic element cannot be completely regulated. Leadership itself has a charismatic dimension, and pastors gain credibility by manifesting the Spirit in their ministry. Effective pastors appear as "genuinely human" and as authentic Christians freed by the Spirit for "unselfish service," in exercising their leadership. Rahner has many practical suggestions for creating a declericalized parish. Ridding themselves of "the trappings of office," pastors should act in an open and transparent way. On matters important to the whole parish, they should make known the dynamics of their decision-making process. Respected pastors have the courage to admit mistakes and change poor decisions. In a declericalized parish, parishioners feel free to take initiative in proposing new directions and implementing new programs that further the mission of the parish. Effective pastors create a climate that empowers parishioners to take responsibility for making the parish a genuine sacrament of the reign of God. The pastoral task is to identify the specific gifts and talents of individual parishioners, facilitate their development, and coordinate them for the good of the parish. This strategy helps develop many diverse energy centers in the parish, multiplying its power to carry on the work of Christ.

The Parish and Social Justice[9]

The local church is a servant community called to work for justice in the world. Sin has invaded social structures that perpetuate systemic evil. Social sin produces false consciousness that blinds whole groups to the injustices endured by oppressed people. In this situation, Rahner warns the clergy against acting like "ecclesiological introverts," more concerned about internal church offices than the human needs of the larger community. He encourages pastors to deal directly with social issues, even when it is unpopular and even detrimental to some parishioners. Sometimes this means presenting "concrete directives about socio-political action" rather than sticking to "colorless principles which upset no one." Realizing that challenging "unjust social situations in a concrete way" will lead to divisions in a parish, Rahner still believes this is better than avoiding conflict by sticking with vague principles. We find examples of Rahner's radical approach in base communities around the world that courageously challenge specific instances of injustice, inspired by Jesus the liberator and Catholic social teaching.

A Parish with Open Doors[10]

Given the pluralism of the modern world, Rahner argues that "we must be a Church with open doors." Today it is harder to decide what constitutes the criteria for church membership. The "theologically relevant frontiers" of the church are "obscure and certainly very fluid." In practice, it is harder to distinguish what really divides those who claim membership in the church and those who don't. While recognizing that the hierarchy has the responsibility to defend orthodoxy and must "forcefully repel heresy," Rahner points out how difficult it is today "to assign exactly the limits of orthodoxy." There is a legitimate theological pluralism within the church. Good Catholics have very different perceptions of the real meaning of key Christian doctrines, including the existence of God. Rahner contends that we should not treat individuals who once left the church and want to return as if they are prodigal sons or lost sheep. On the contrary, Christian charity calls us to treat these "marginal settlers" as brothers and sisters who may have all along maintained a spiritual relationship to the church, perhaps even deeper than those who never left. This line of argument also supports an open-door policy for those wishing to join the church. Pastors should not impose on them stricter criteria for membership than governs current members. If they have trouble accepting a particular doctrine, like the immaculate conception, it is sufficient for them to stay open to the possibility that it will have meaning for them as their spiritual journey continues. This pastoral strategy has enabled many good people with genuine Catholic sensibilities to join the church despite some carefully considered reservations. Finally, the open-door approach enables many Catholics to remain in the church despite difficulties accepting every part of the Catholic symbol system. In one sense, all members of the church are "cafeteria Catholics" since no one personally appropriates everything in the long and rich Catholic tradition. Many Catholics, for instance, affirm the Nicene Creed without understanding Christ's descent into hell or finding spiritual meaning in it. Rahner's open-door theology has special pastoral relevance in our postmodern world where it is hard to master such great pluralism and complexity in all areas of life, including questions of church membership.

An Open Parish[11]

Rahner argues not only for an open-door policy but also for "an open church" that stays engaged with the world. He feared a "ghetto mentality" in the post–Vatican II church that tends to withdraw from "the public life of society," reducing the church to what sociologists consider a sect. Catholics who favor a sectarian church see the world as an evil place to be kept at a distance, with "as many taboos as possible." They tend to think of Catholics who favor a more open posture toward the world as enemies of orthodoxy. Actually, it is more obvious today that the church cannot be reduced to a sect based on some strict standards of orthodoxy, because of the great pluralism already present in the Catholic community. The Catholic Church is by its very nature an open church called to evangelize individuals and to promote societal justice and peace.

The open church is actualized in local parishes. Healthy parishes resist the sectarian temptation to turn inward. Instead, they concentrate on engaging the world in diverse ways. For example, parishioners attuned to their baptismal call attempt to live the Gospel at the worksite and in the civic community. Preachers regularly highlight the social justice implications of the liturgical readings. The parish promotes Christian service projects that involve personal interaction with the needy and theological reflection on the whole activity. Parish volunteers collect food and serve it at a local food distribution center. The social justice committee keeps the whole parish aware of local and national issues, always looking for ways to organize a collaborative response to them. At Mass, the prayer of the faithful includes petitions for those in need locally and around the world. Some parishioners participate in direct action, including civil disobedience, to protest injustice. Pastors create an atmosphere that celebrates the open church and encourages parishioners to use their unique gifts to counter the demonic tendencies in the world and to cooperate with God's grace in building the kingdom. This sketch of an ideal open parish suggests possibilities for real parishes looking for ways to help humanize the culture and transform society. The open engaged church model has received a great boost from Pope Francis through his example and his repeated reminders that the church confined to the sanctuary suffocates but regains energy in reaching out to those in need.

The Parish and Spirituality[12]

The parish should be a community that nourishes the spiritual life of all its members. Rahner recognized that parish life can be spiritually lifeless—dominated by ritualism, legalism, and a "resigned spiritual mediocrity." He thought pastors confined to a church environment could become out of touch with the real-life struggles of their parishioners. According to Rahner, clergy should at least try to imagine the challenges their parishioners face in living a normal secular life. Rahner wanted pastors to reflect on how to present the Christian message in a credible way that had meaning for secularized people, "living as satisfied members of the consumer society." Parish leaders must avoid glib talk about weighty life concerns: for example, offering premature consolation to people still immersed in the early stages of grief for the loss of a loved one. Vibrant parishes promote conversation about spiritual concerns: sharing favorite images of God; witnessing to the significance of Jesus in daily life; celebrating the joy of the Holy Spirit present in stressful situations; keeping the commandments of God not as a burdensome duty but a glorious liberation from fear and egotism; reflecting on the classic spiritual writings; participating in the struggle for greater justice and peace; maintaining a contemplative spirit in the midst of busy demanding days; managing anxiety over death; and keeping hope alive on dark days. Honest conversations, formal and informal, on these kinds of questions enrich parish life. Pastors who participate in such discussions are prepared to present homilies that address real concerns and reflect the wisdom of ordinary people. Parish organizations and programs should include a spiritual dimension that provides perspective, motivation, and direction. The experience of parishioners living out Christian ideals in the real world helps make the parish a richer spiritual resource.

Ecumenical Concerns[13]

A parish should contribute at the local level to the ecumenical movement that strives to overcome divisions among Christians and achieve the unity Christ desired for his followers. Near the end of his life, Rahner argued that theologians had cleared away the doctrinal obstacles to the reunion of Catholics and mainline Protestants so that the churches could actually unite in the near future. He made the point that there would be no more diversity in the reconciled church than already exists in the Catholic Church. Three decades later, we still do not have the kind of unity Jesus prayed for in his farewell discourse at the Last Supper. This is the case despite continuing progress at the theological level, including the historic 1999 *Joint Declaration on the Doctrine of Justification* issued by the Lutheran World Federation and the Catholic Church. This lack of progress at the institutional level has made it difficult to sustain the passion for Christian unity that was so alive in the early years after Vatican II.

Given the decline in ecumenical passion, parishes should put more emphasis on keeping alive the dream of a reconciled unity among Christian communities. Many parish activities could include an ecumenical dimension: for example, cooperating with another church in running a food distribution center for the poor. Developing an ecumenical spirit in the parish alerts parishioners to their responsibility to create friendly relations with their Christian neighbors and colleagues. Current practices suggest many opportunities for mutual interactions: periodic pulpit exchanges, common services on special days like Good Friday and Thanksgiving, regular meetings of congregational leaders, prayers for other churches at Sunday liturgies, and collaborative efforts on common local problems such as racism and poverty. The hope remains that parish-based grassroots ecumenism, grounded in solid theological principles, will eventually move church leaders to take positive steps toward institutional unity.

Parish as Voluntary Association[14]

Rahner foresaw that parishes in the future would take on more characteristics of voluntary associations. Many Catholics would no longer belong to parishes simply because of social expectations or the example of parents. People today, especially the millennial generation, make decisions about church affiliation based on which parish best meets their spiritual needs. Attending parishes outside geographical boundaries is now common and an accepted practice. This sets up a competitive situation, even if denied or undervalued by pastors, which highlights the need for competent, dedicated parish leaders. In this regard, Rahner offered a radical solution: parishes could surface the real leaders of the faith community; provide them with the necessary education and present them to the bishop for ordination. This would help overcome two serious problems: the shortage of priests and the inability of some priests to be effective leaders. Under the current system, a man who has no real leadership skills or ability to preach effectively can apply to the seminary, receive training, and be ordained. He is then assigned to a parish, leaving the parish with a priest who is presumably of good will but lacks the ability to provide effective leadership. Rahner's proposal offers a better chance that the pastor will be an effective leader. It also solves the priest shortage problem by assuring every viable Christian community a process for discerning and securing a priest to serve them. Furthermore, Rahner maintained that the real leader could be married or unmarried and that in the modern Western world there is no reason why the leader could not be a woman. He argued that there is no good historical or theological reason for forbidding the ordination of women, and, therefore, freedom should prevail, allowing for women's ordination to become a legitimate development within the church. He rejected the argument that Jesus picked only males as members of the Twelve on the grounds that prevailing social custom made it impossible for women to serve as public witnesses to anything including the public ministry of Jesus.[15]

Creative Leadership

With a growing number of Catholics attending parishes of choice, pastoral leaders have added incentive for providing good service.[16] Parishes attract people in a variety of ways: being welcoming communities; providing prayerful liturgies with relevant homilies and singable music; offering a variety of solid religious education opportunities; organizing support groups for parishioners dealing with divorce, grief, and other challenges; attending to those who are sick and grieving; encouraging personal and group efforts on behalf of justice and peace; eliciting advice and suggestions on matters of common concern; and allowing parishioners opportunities to voice their grievances. Attractive parishes tap the talents and interests of parishioners by offering opportunities to participate in various structured groups such as parish councils, liturgy committees, finance councils, marriage preparation teams, and social justice committees.

Pastoral leaders help attract people by being open, approachable, caring, competent, and especially by loving the people they serve. Pastoral teams can appeal to more people if they represent age and gender diversity, while sharing a common vision of the parish mission. Given the current situation, it is especially important to find creative ways for women to participate more fully in parish leadership. Further possibilities can build on the great ministry already being done by women who today constitute a substantial majority of lay ecclesial ministers. Wise pastors serve more effectively by recognizing their own strengths and limitations. For example, a poor preacher could find ways to have more witness talks at Mass; a good teacher could do many of the classes in the RCIA program; an unorganized pastor could hire a competent pastoral administrator; a pastor who has trouble relating to the sick could delegate this to the parish deacon; and a priest with a broad vision could write the parish mission statement rather than the committee assigned this task. Such wise sharing of responsibilities helps make a parish more attractive to Catholics shopping for a spiritual home.

In the United States we are blessed with many fine parishes that are genuine sacraments of the risen Lord and effective signs of the kingdom. Creative pastoral leaders have found ways to adapt the vision of Vatican II to very diverse situations in our country. They have gained the trust of their parishioners and empowered them to use their specific gifts for the common good. They have energized the congregation around major projects like establishing an adult education program or forming partnerships to improve the neighborhood. In the process, they have relied on the Spirit and demonstrated that pastoral ministry is more of a creative art than a technical strategy.

Summary

Rahner's ecclesiology, which sees the church as an event and the parish as an actualization of the universal church, provides a solid theological basis for a broad understanding of parish ministry. His theological vision prompts creative planning on the part of pastoral ministers who are accustomed to thinking of the church as a set institution. Some pastoral leaders may see Rahner's many pastoral suggestions for improving parish life as an affirmation of ministry already well done. Others may use them as a catalyst for new initiatives to revitalize the parish. His more radical suggestions, which seem so distant, can at least keep alive hopes for a better future.

Personal Reflections: Exemplifying Rahner's Pastoral Influence

Introduction

The psychotherapist Carl Rogers famously claimed that when we speak most personally, we speak most universally. This chapter describes Karl Rahner's influence on me and my five decades of priestly ministry in the hope that it will strike responsive chords with others. In part, this is a restatement of fundamental ideas from the first four chapters on anthropology, God, Christ, and church, placed in the context of my personal experience. Some of my recent "Reflections" articles are included in this chapter to illustrate various ways Rahner has influenced my ministry.[1]

Discovering Rahner

During my seminary studies of theology from 1958 to 1962, I do not recall ever hearing the name Karl Rahner even mentioned. For certain, I knew absolutely nothing about him or his thought. Shortly after my ordination in 1962 for the Diocese of Toledo, while serving as an assistant pastor at St. Mary's Church in Sandusky, Ohio, I was asked to give a talk to a local Kiwanis Club. In searching for material for the talk, I accidentally came across a book by Karl Rahner titled *Theology for Renewal*. Paging through it, I discovered a chapter on men in the church that caught my eye because I was addressing an all-male audience. Parts of the chapter were hard for me to understand, but one idea struck me: men are commonly reluctant to speak openly about God and deep matters of the heart. My talk to the Kiwanis Club based on Rahner's insight went over very well and drew a number of positive responses. It was the first time I recognized that the work of theologians could be pastorally helpful, and it began a lifelong engagement with the theology of Karl Rahner. Over the years, I grew to appreciate the importance of Rahner's contention that the more theology appropriates the diverse richness of the Christian tradition and relates it to the deep questions posed by contemporary culture, the more spiritually and pastorally relevant it will be.

Pastoral Guidance

My initial positive encounter with Rahner's theology led me to the regular practice of turning to him for help in meeting my pastoral responsibilities. Assigned to teach a sophomore religion class on liturgy in the parish high school, I made use of Rahner's understanding of sacraments as both actualizations of the church and encounters with the risen Christ. Rahner's insightful work on the sacrament of penance helped enrich the many hours spent every Saturday in the confessional during my early years as a priest. He guided me to recognize frequent confessions of devotion as opportunities for spiritual growth and led me to the practice—which I still employ—of discussing with the penitent the most appropriate penance for making progress as a disciple of Christ.

Over the years, Catholics have developed various ways of celebrating the sacrament of penance. Individuals tend to go to confession less frequently but with more meaning. Most of my parishioners prefer going face-to-face and often are looking for spiritual guidance. They tend to talk about progress as well as setbacks on the spiritual journey. Many confess in terms of sinful patterns rather than reciting a long list of sins. Central to the process is the proclamation of God's mercy expressed by the priest and officially articulated in the official prayer of absolution. The whole notion of forgiveness is essential to the message of Jesus. No other spiritual teacher has understood as well as Christ the crucial role forgiveness plays in human affairs. My experience of the power of God's forgiving mercy present in the sacrament of penance stands behind this reflection.

Forgiveness and the Prodigal Son Parable

The Prodigal Son parable (Luke 15:11-32) contains profound insights on the issue of forgiveness, which is crucial for personal growth and communal harmony. The general story line is familiar: the younger son gets his father to give him his share of the estate and goes off to a distant country where he squanders the money on a life of dissipation and ends up destitute; he decides to return home to work as a hired hand for his father; seeing him coming, the father runs out to greet him, embraces him, and throws a great feast for him; the older son is upset and refuses to enter the party; the father pleads with him to join the celebration because his brother was lost and has been found.

Much of the power of the parable comes from the moral authority of the storyteller. According to Luke, Jesus told the story in response to the scribes and Pharisees who accused him of associating with sinners. The message of the parable is consistent with his general teaching on forgiveness as well as his personal example. He instructed his disciples to forgive their enemies and, while suffering the cruel torments of crucifixion, asked his Father to forgive his executioners. In accord with his message of divine mercy, Jesus saved the woman taken in adultery from stoning and forgave her sins. After his resurrection, he greeted the disciples who had abandoned him with the reconciling words: "Peace be with you." In the life of Jesus, the power of forgiveness to facilitate spiritual growth and create harmonious relationships is revealed with a striking depth and clarity.

Christians try to appropriate Christ's message of forgiveness from within the perspective of faith. Individuals outside the circle of explicit faith have also recognized the unique contribution of Jesus in this area. For example, the secular Jewish philosopher Hannah Arendt declared: "The discoverer of the role of forgiveness in the realm of human affairs was Jesus of Nazareth." His discovery has implications for the whole human family, including the more secularized members, because "the faculty of forgiving" is the only possible way out of "the predicament of irreversibility" caused by human misdeeds. In Christian terms, the grace of forgiveness is the only way to rise above the estrangement caused by sin and to move forward the kingdom ideal of integration and harmony. The Prodigal Son parable carries extra significance and power because it represents the message of Jesus, the master of forgiveness.

In the first act of the parable, the younger son seeks and obtains his share of the father's estate and goes off to a distant land. Modern readers can interpret the son's behavior in various positive ways: taking initiative to better himself; seeking his fortune; beginning a process of self-discovery; getting out on his own; making his own way in life. In the original setting of the story, however, his decision to take his portion and depart is clearly reprehensible and destructive. He cut himself off from his family and exposed his father to public ridicule for violating the common wisdom that a father should not share his estate while still alive.

The son's sinful decision led to a moral freefall. He squandered his inheritance in a wild life of dissipation that included soliciting prostitutes. His personal degradation reached a low point when he, as a Jew, was forced to work for a Gentile at the most distasteful of tasks, tending swine. Coming to his senses, he recognized that he had sinned against God and his father. In his own heart, he felt he was no longer worthy to be called his father's son. He decided to return home, confess his sins to his father, and ask to be treated as a hired worker.

The younger son invites us to come to our senses, to engage in a sincere examination of conscience about our own need for forgiveness. The call is to set aside rationalization and self-deception in favor of a self-critical assessment of the particular ways we have failed to love God and our neighbor. Belief in God's great love and mercy prompts an honest examination of conscience. We can admit our sinfulness because forgiveness is available in overflowing abundance. We do not have a claim on this divine mercy or a strict right to divine pardon. Forgiveness appears as a gift, which prompts a grateful effort to make amends and to offer proper reparation for our sins.

In the parable, the father caught sight of his returning son while he was still a long way off. He ran to his son, embraced him, kissed him, clothed him with the finest garments, and ordered a great celebration for his son who was dead and had come to life again. Despite his son's selfish decision to leave the family, the father did not disown him or block him from memory. Quite the contrary, he maintained the relationship and kept his son in his heart and mind. Although the prodigal felt he was no longer worthy to be called a son, the father never doubted the reality of their relationship because he knew it did not ultimately depend on proper behavior. Although his son departed from the family home, the father knew in his heart that the bonds of blood and spirit that held them together were deeper and stronger than physical separation and personal misdeeds.

In the book Exclusion and Embrace, *Miroslav Volf offers an insightful analysis of the father's embrace of his younger son. In opening wide his arms, the father signals his acceptance and forgiveness of his son. He waits for his son to respond, hoping his guilt will not cloud his memory of their relationship. When his son accepts the invitation, the father closes his arms in an embrace, which demonstrates respect and care. Finally, the father opens his arms, encouraging his son to regain his identity and to construct a new life so that they can now relate on the basis of mutuality, respect, and love.*

Reflection on the forgiving father can lead us into the mystery of divine mercy. The God revealed by Jesus is Unconditional Love, merciful beyond human imagining, more forgiving than the most compassionate of human fathers. This God seeks out sinners, grants them the grace of repentance and restores in them the gift of divine life. Our God does not imprison us in our past sinfulness but offers us new opportunities to cooperate with grace in living a more virtuous life. No sin is beyond forgiveness; no repentant sinner is rejected. The celebratory feast initiated by the return of the prodigal reinforces the teaching of Jesus that there is joy in heaven over the repentance of sinners.

Some readers of the parable get more engaged in the second act of the story and identify with the older son who is angry with his father and refuses to go to his brother's party. He is hurt because his father never had a party for him, even though he has been a faithful, hardworking son. He is resentful of his brother who blew his inheritance on prostitutes and now enjoys this big celebration. Most of us recognize the temptation to boycott the party. We know the kind of anger, hurt, and resentment that hardens the heart. Sometimes forgiveness seems like a betrayal of values, a violation of justice, an easy accommodation with sin.

The father tries to explain to his older son the deep truths that can soften his heart and cleanse his soul. Relationships are more important than misdeeds. Despite his mistakes, my son is still your brother. Even though you are angry with me now, you are still my son and everything that I have is yours. There is no injustice here. Your brother has indeed squandered his share of the inheritance, and he will get no part of what is coming to you. We must celebrate, however, because your brother who was dead has come to life again.

The father's wise words prompt further reflection on the art of forgive-
ness. Hardness of heart is dangerous to our health. Resentment can poison
our system and forgiveness is the only reliable antidote. As some psycholo-
gists have suggested, we can find greater inner peace by changing our
role in grievance stories from the perpetual victim who keeps replaying
the hurt to the noble hero who graciously forgives and lives with greater
freedom and energy. From a Christian perspective, individuals are more
than their misdeeds and sins. They are made in God's image and have an
inherent worth that cannot be totally obliterated by sin. Since God has
forgiven us, we have a responsibility to share that gift with others. For-
giveness is not the same as forgetting, nor does it imply acceptance of
sinful behavior. It does mean giving offenders the chance to begin again,
to construct a better story, to demonstrate that there is more to them than
their sins. Human affairs go better when we follow the example of the
merciful Jesus and heed his call to love our enemies and to pray for those
who hurt us (Matt 5:44).

Dealing with Suffering and Death[2]

In the important and often challenging ministerial tasks connected
with death (visiting the sick, comforting the dying, burying the dead,
and attending to the grieving), I find helpful perspectives and insights
in Rahner's theology of death that calls us to face our own death with
a sober realism and with Christian hope. Especially significant is
Rahner's notion that death is not simply a separation of body and
soul passively endured but a free act of handing ourselves over to
the loving God, making definitive and irrevocable our fundamental
option for good over evil. Pastorally, Rahner guides me to speak
openly with the critically ill about death and to avoid glib talk with
those grieving the loss of loved ones. When I first met Rahner, he
asked me, after a lengthy conversation, to pray for his happy death.
Over time, I came to realize that this strange request reflected his own
anxiety about death and his keen sense of sadness over the loss of
loved ones. His profound prayer "God of the Living," found in his
Prayers for a Lifetime, reveals both his struggles and his faith. He begins
by recognizing that "there are no others who can fill the vacancy
when one of those whom I have really loved suddenly and unexpect-
edly departs and is with me no more." His sense of loss is frustrating:

"They have gone away: they are silent. Not a word comes from them; not a single sign of their gentle love and kindness comes to warm my heart." To assuage his doubts, he turns to God for a sign: "But why am I asking this of You? You are as silent to me as my dead." And then a moment of recognition: "I know why You are silent: Your silence is the framework of my faith, the boundless space where my love finds the strength to believe in Your Love." And finally a statement of hope: "My dead live the unhampered and limitless Life that You live; they love with Your Love; and thus their life and their love no longer fit into the frail and narrow forms of my present existence."

When my mother died a number of years ago, I wrote about her as a great example of Rahner's idea that acceptance is at the center of Christian spirituality.

A Spirituality of Acceptance

My mother, Lillian Marie Noble Bacik, spent Lent this year preparing for an irrevocable Easter encounter with the risen Lord. During this time, I joined my sisters, Barbara and Patricia, in caring for our mother in her own home. Our goal was to surround her with love and to keep her comfortable with the expert assistance of Hospice of Northwest Ohio. As my mother got progressively weaker, I tried, on one occasion, to commiserate with her: "Mom, you don't have control over very much anymore." She replied knowingly: "That is right. I don't have control over anything. And, James, neither do you." My mother, who remained a wise spiritual guide for me to the very end, had a remarkable ability to accept the realities of life, including the crosses that came her way.

According to Karl Rahner, acceptance is the key to the Christian life. For him, striving to achieve self-acceptance, in all its various dimensions and aspects, is crucial to spiritual growth. We can think of acceptance as a Christian virtue inclining us to submit to the Father's will, to take up our cross and follow Christ, and to acknowledge the Spirit as the source of all good gifts. It moves us to recognize ourselves as social, interdependent beings who find our fulfillment in serving others. Acceptance prompts us to stay immersed in the real world with its mixture of grace and sin, joys and sorrows, hopes and frustrations. It is opposed to cheap grace, utopian plans, easy answers, weak passivity, and all forms of escapism.

Full acceptance is difficult to achieve. Many of us have trouble accepting the crosses of life: suffering, diminishment, loss, failure, sickness, the death of loved ones. Others seem incapable of recognizing blessings and graces, burdened as they are by cynicism or depression. The proud have trouble accepting faults, failings, limitations, and sins; while those with poor self-esteem cannot recognize virtues, accomplishments, and successes. All of us know the temptation to exclude those who are different, to prejudge others, to stereotype groups, to make unfair comparisons, and to see the speck in our neighbor's eye while ignoring the beam in our own. Some believers have trouble accepting their accountability before God, while others struggle to accept God's merciful forgiveness. Finally, there is always the danger that acceptance will lead to passivity, to a false sense of resignation that too easily tolerates evil and submits to injustice.

To cultivate the virtue of acceptance, we Christians instinctively turn to Jesus Christ for guidance and strength. Jesus was totally committed to doing the will of his Father and to working for the cause of humanity. Throughout his public life, he refused to turn stones into bread by taking the easy way out. He resisted the temptation to jump down from the top of the temple, and chose instead the demanding path of going about doing good day by day. Despite the objections of his disciples, his sense of dedication took him to Jerusalem where enemies sought his life. Sensing cruel and mortal danger, he prayed alone in the garden that this cup of suffering would pass him by but then added a grand and memorable statement of acceptance: "Not my will but yours be done" (Luke 22:42). Strengthened by prayer, Jesus took up his cross, providing his disciples in all ages with motivation for shouldering the arduous, sweaty, messy, complex task of spreading the reign of justice and peace in the world.

My own personal sense of the meaning and power of acceptance comes from my mother, Lillian Bacik. She was especially good at graciously accepting the crosses that came her way throughout her long life. Her piety was shaped by the devotional Catholicism of her German ethnic background, which focused on the sufferings of Christ in his passion and death. This spirituality drew inspiration from a variety of devotional practices, including strict Lenten observances, Stations of the Cross, parish missions, Marian novenas, and the rosary. It helped strengthen immigrant Catholics for the struggle to enter the mainstream of American life.

My mother's faith was tested when her third child, David, was born with the Rh factor, which totally arrested his normal development. As it became clear that there was no medical cure, she experienced the tempta-

tion to blame God for this reversal of good fortune or to blame herself for producing a defective child. At that point, guided by her pastor, she made an explicit conscious decision not to cast blame but to accept her role as mother of a son who needed total care. For the next seven years, she devoted herself to this task with love and compassion and without complaint or bitterness, until demands on her time and energy forced her to place my brother in the care of professionals—the most difficult decision of her life, which demanded another type of acceptance, this time of personal limitation.

There was a gritty toughness in my mother's sense of acceptance, which colored her approach to child rearing. As a little kid, I wanted to go to a neighboring playground to play baseball but was afraid to pass through an area where some tough kids might beat me up. I presented my dilemma to my mom, expecting that she would take me to the playground. Her response was that if I wanted to play ball, I would have to get myself over there. In word and example, she repeated that fundamental message many times over—you have to face reality and cannot expect an easy way out.

On April 17, 1979, my father suffered a stroke and was taken to the hospital. As I held my mother and my sister Pat, the doctor told us that he could not survive in any fully human state. My knees buckled and I suggested we pray that the Lord take him, but my mother quickly insisted that we pray to accept whatever happened: for strength to care for him if he lingered and for courage to deal with our loss if he died. I later asked my mother how she could be so much wiser than her theologian son at that critical moment, and she replied that she simply was in the habit of always praying for acceptance. She did not ask God, for example, that her children would turn out a certain way but that she could accept us as we actually developed. Thus, I came to understand something of the wellspring of my mother's virtue of acceptance—trust in God nourished by regular and consistent prayer.

My father died soon after his stroke, and for the next twenty-three years, I periodically heard his voice reminding me to take good care of my mother—the woman he loved so much. This was an easy task because I enjoyed spending time with her at meals, concerts, and sporting events, or watching a serious program on television. She was pleasant to be with, never demanding, always understanding, and interested in a wide variety of topics. On one occasion, I took her out to eat and noticed she was favoring her left arm. Over her protests, I took her to a doctor who diagnosed *a severely cracked elbow and put her arm in a soft case with the admonition that she would need around-the-clock care. Driving her home, I fretted about how to provide this constant care. Without saying much, she went into the kitchen and opened a jar, then successfully handled going to the bathroom by herself, and then got into her car and drove around the block, with me as a passenger, after which she announced with quiet assurance: "I guess I won't need constant care." In her seventies, my mother still had the gritty determination to accept the hardships of life and to carry her crosses gracefully.*

Lillian Bacik was also very good at accepting other people in their unique individuality. She was amazingly nonjudgmental and seldom compared one person to another. If someone paid one of her children a compliment, her standard response was, "I am proud of all my children." She did not set up expectations or demand predetermined responses. One son-in-law said she was absolutely the most accepting human being he ever encountered. Her accepting attitude turned our home into an "oasis of peace," as my sister Barbara called it, a place of hospitality where our friends felt welcome. A number of people thought of her as their second mother, including some who did not feel accepted in their own family. Comments at my mother's funeral reinforced my perception that her gift of acceptance radiated a remarkable liberating power, enabling individuals to see themselves more positively and to accept their own distinctive gifts. A friend of mine, who spent Thanksgiving Day at my parents' home many years ago, told me it was a liberating and even life-changing experience for her. Simply summarized, her own parents weighed her down with constant expectations, while my mother freed her up by giving her permission to be herself.

Lee Bacik was not as good at accepting her own gifts and talents. I treasured her logical mind, remarkable memory, and keen insights, as well as the wisdom she gained from long experience. When I periodically told her how her ideas and experiences helped individuals in my parish, she would deflect the compliment in various ways, including the correct, but incomplete, comment that any good accomplished was really God's work. I often thought, but never said, that God does accomplish good through human beings like her.

The acceptance that my mother consistently cultivated through her adult life came into special play during the last month of her life as she became more and more dependent on her children. She was beautifully gracious to all her visitors, although she had no trouble telling them when it was time for them to go. For every act of kindness and service, she had a word or gesture of gratitude, except for the time when my assistance was especially clumsy, and she said she was sending me back for further nurses' training. We celebrated home Masses, shared the anointing of the sick, offered the prayers for the dying, and kept our nightly ritual of medicine and prayers. Near the end, when my sister Barbara told her we hoped that she felt surrounded by love, she whispered her last words: "I do, I do"—a comforting assurance from a deeply loved mother, who prayed all her life for the gift of acceptance.

Priest Retreats

In directing retreats for priests, I draw on Rahner's understanding of the priest as servant leader and proclaimer of the Word. He reminds us that priests are not angels sent from God but men chosen from among the ranks of the baptized to serve the community. As priests, we speak not our own words but the word of God. Our ministry is important because the community needs to hear that God's mercy is stronger than sin and that eternal life triumphs over death. Rahner helps priests deal with personal limitations and ministerial failures by reminding us that no one is required to do the impossible and that our task is to empower others. His theology prompts us to be on alert for clues to the presence of the Spirit in the lives of all the people we meet and serve. In empowering others and contemplating their stories, priests often experience a surprising vitality and profound sense of gratitude.

In addressing priests, I am always looking for ways of understanding the different approaches to the priesthood operative today. The following analysis has struck a responsive chord with many laypersons as well as priests.

Two Models of the Priesthood

We can discern two models of the priesthood operative in the Catholic Church today: the servant-leader model that reflects the teaching of the Second Vatican Council and the spiritual father model inspired by the example and teaching of Pope John Paul II. Achieving a deeper under-standing of these models can be an important step toward overcoming the unfortunate polarization that continues to undermine the mission of the church.

World War II helped move Catholics in the United States into a new social position that played a role in the development of the servant-leader model. The war brought Catholics out of their religious ghettos and into contact with other citizens serving in the military and working in defense industries. After the war, the G.I. Bill enabled Catholics to go to college in large numbers. As a result, they were able to get good jobs previously denied to Catholics and move out of their enclaves into the suburbs, where they helped establish new parishes. The election of John F. Kennedy in 1960 as the first Catholic president signaled the entrance of the Catholic community as a whole into the mainstream of the political, economic, and social life of the country.

Immigrant Catholics living on the margins held their priests in high regard for providing them with the sacraments and for helping them cope with an often hostile world. As Catholics moved into the mainstream, pastors faced the challenging task of ministering to parishioners who were more affluent, better educated, and generally more attuned to the ideals of a pluralistic democracy. Seminary training did not prepare priests for this new type of ministry, and the classic model of the priesthood that served the immigrants so well proved to be inadequate.

In this situation, Vatican II was a special blessing for the church in the United States. The council did not produce a comprehensive theology of the priesthood, but it did enunciate themes that helped create the servant-leader model. By baptism, all Christians share in the priesthood of Christ. All are called to holiness, and all share in the task of building up the Body of Christ and spreading his kingdom in the world. Liturgy demands the full, active, and conscious participation of the whole as-sembly. Christians share the joys and hopes of the human family and have the responsibility to work for justice and peace in the world. Priests have the responsibility of pastoral care for the faith community and are not limited to the cultic role of offering sacrifice. Pastors are to learn from the example of Jesus, who came not to be served but to serve. They act sacra-mentally in the person of Christ, the head of the church. They must not quench the Spirit but "must discover with faith, recognize with joy and foster with diligence the many charismatic gifts of the laity whether these be humble or exciting" (PO 9).

Priests who took responsibility for implementing the directives of Vatican II and found creative ways of serving a more active and educated laity gradually developed what we now call the "servant-leader model." This model encourages pastors to form close relationships with parishioners: listening to them and learning from them, celebrating their gifts and empowering them to use them to build up the Body of Christ, providing them with liturgy where all play their proper roles, reminding them to carry out their mission to humanize the world, and sharing with them the common call to follow Christ. For parishioners, this model gives expression to their hopes for priests who are authentic human beings, committed Christians, and effective overseers dedicated to following the example of Christ.

By the 1990s, a new approach to the priesthood in the United States had developed that can be called "the spiritual father" model. It is, in large measure, a reaction to what some critics perceive as unfortunate ongoing trends in the post–Vatican II church: losing a clear sense of Catholic identity, conceding too much to the secular culture, watering down Catholic teaching, settling for a moral relativism, and reducing the sense of mystery in the liturgy. Some Catholics resonate with the claim that liberal interpretations of Vatican II produced a "beige Catholicism" that demands a new mission to reclaim a clear, distinctive, colorful Catholic identity. For them, this mission is especially important today, since traditional religion is involved in "a culture war" against legal abortion, gay marriage, rampant divorce, and illegal drugs. In this war, we need a more aggressive expression of Catholicism.

Through his compelling example and authoritative writing, Pope John Paul II suggested a distinctive way of following the priestly vocation. He fully accepted and endorsed the teaching of Vatican II on the priesthood but gave it enough of his own personal slant to suggest a new model. For example, while accepting the conciliar teaching on the baptismal priesthood, he stressed that the ordained priesthood is essentially different. The sacrament of holy orders confers a special character that changes the very being of a priest so that he participates ontologically in the priesthood of Christ. The call to priesthood is a free gift from God mediated through the church and not a right that would open up the priesthood to women. The principal task of priests is to offer the sacrifice of the Mass. The priest is not only "a man of the Eucharist" but also "a man of the sacred" with a special vocation to holiness. The pope strongly defended celibacy as "a sacred charism" and a sign of priestly commitment. He opposed priests getting directly involved in political activities because this is not the proper role of the clergy and infringes on the mission of the laity to humanize social structures. In short, John Paul viewed the priest as "a spiritual father," called to give life and guidance to the members of the church.

Compared to servant leaders, priests today who see themselves as spiritual fathers tend to be more confident that they have a clear teaching to impart. They are more interested in handing on a distinctive Catholic identity, more committed to teaching parishioners than learning from them, more taken with the uniqueness of the ordained priesthood in relation to the baptismal priesthood, more concerned about building up the church than in humanizing the world, more disposed to oppose abortion than to support the consistent ethic of life, more concerned about internal church matters than ecumenical or interfaith dialogue, and more likely to wear distinctive clerical garb.

Parishioners who favor this model tend to have certain expectations of their pastors: that they preach and teach orthodox Catholicism, stand up boldly for a clear Catholic identity, are a firm voice against abortion, and act as "other Christs" in leading the parish.

A better understanding of the dynamics of the servant-leader and spiritual father models suggests guidelines for dialogue with those on the other side: get to know them as individuals and not as types, assume their good will and resist the temptation to demonize them, allow them to define themselves and do not impose a stereotype on them, consider their strengths and not only their weaknesses, and highlight successful collaboration with them and not just the tensions. Respectful dialogue helps free both servant-leaders and spiritual fathers to concentrate on their ministerial responsibilities. No individual priests will fit perfectly into either model. Some priests will manifest traits of both, while others will find new, creative ways of ministering. History will reveal which approaches prove the most effective in meeting the distinctive challenges of the postmodern world.

Religious Education

In 1967, my bishop sent me to Fordham for two years to get a graduate degree in religious education. At that time, New York was a great center of theological activity. I was able to take classes from outstanding scholars who were visiting professors at Union Theological: Ray Brown, the great Catholic biblical scholar who lectured on the death of the Messiah; Hans Kung, already well known for his book on the council, who taught a course on ecumenical sacramentology and gave a series of public lectures on church reform; and John Macquarrie, the Anglican theologian who lectured on contemporary theology and later directed my dissertation at Oxford where he held an endowed chair. I had the opportunity to attend public lectures by the Canadian Jesuit Bernard Lonergan and the Dutch Dominican Edward Schillebeeckx, which exposed me to the great ferment going on in Catholic theology.

During my second year in New York, I worked as an assistant to Gabriel Moran at Manhattan College. A marvelous classroom teacher, Moran had just published his *Theology of Revelation* and a companion volume, *Catechesis of Revelation*. His work, greatly influenced by Karl Rahner, gave me a deeper understanding of the way theology can guide pastoral practice. Moran insisted that all religious education should have an adult focus, which means providing a great variety of opportunities for adults to deepen their faith as well as encouraging young people to become lifelong learners. For Moran, religion courses at all levels should be taught in an academically sound way, with emphasis on understanding the content of the faith. At the same time, there was a countertrend in Catholic catechetics that stressed process over content and favored open discussion of relevant topics over a systematic presentation of Catholic doctrine. Unfortunately, Moran's approach did not prevail around the country, and we ended up with many Catholics lacking a theologically solid understanding of their faith.

As a result of my time with Moran, I became a great advocate of adult religious education and looked for ways to accomplish this at the parish level. In teaching adults after the council, the need for reinterpreting Catholic teaching became more evident to me. Once again, Rahner's work of reinterpreting traditional scholastic theology in a modern context proved to be extremely helpful. Older Catholics, questioning what they learned in their youth, often find Rahner's explanations of traditional teachings more intelligible and credible. Many of my "Reflections" articles drew on Rahnerian reinterpretations, as did the following.

Reinterpreting Original Sin

If non-Christians can receive the gift of eternal happiness, as Vatican II taught, and if unbaptized babies can enjoy the beatific vision, as Pope Benedict and the International Theological Commission suggested, then we need to rethink the popular understanding of original sin as a stain on the soul that can only be washed away by the waters of baptism. Many Christians who simply assume that God will save their good Jewish, Muslim, and Hindu friends as well as unbaptized infants still need a reinterpretation of original sin that respects the council's salvation optimism and fits into a coherent Christian understanding of human existence.

The influential theologian Karl Rahner claims that we can only come to a proper understanding of original sin by keeping in mind the more powerful operation of divine grace in world history and our personal lives. We can understand the first Adam properly only in reference to the second Adam, Jesus Christ. The death and resurrection of the Lord reveals the true nature of the Fall and its consequences. In his masterful work The Joy of Being Wrong: Original Sin Through Easter Eyes, *priest-theologian James Alison applies the Rahnerian approach in a creative and insightful way. For Alison, the resurrection of Jesus, the crucified and forgiving victim, reveals a God of absolute and unconditional love. God is self-giving love, and in God there is no wrath, no vengeance, no death. The Scripture passages that speak of a vengeful God must be interpreted within a framework that consistently upholds God as all-loving and recognizes the human propensity to attribute the dark side of human nature to God.*

From this viewpoint, we cannot imagine the merciful God punishing all human beings for the sin of the first parents and demanding the cruel death of Jesus to pay for the infinite offense against the divine glory. The God who raised Jesus has always willed the salvation of all people and has never been complicit in violence.

Alison also suggests that the resurrection reveals the true nature of human existence and supplies the energy for the new creation. We human beings are essentially relational creatures, always responsive to others. As Augustine understood so well, our hearts are restless and our passionate longings are ambivalent. We are called to channel our energy in constructive ways: to forgive rather than seek vengeance, to include rather than exclude others, to develop relationships on the basis of mutuality rather than rivalry, to help victims rather than victimizing others. The Gospel summons us to structure our desires according to the Lord's teaching and example that were vindicated by his resurrection. The risen Christ also empowers us to create a new human community of justice and peace based on forgiveness and compassion. These kingdom ideals reveal the destructive character of societies driven by patterns of envy and recrimination. The Spirit unleashed by the risen Christ challenges the false consciousness that is blind to the plight of the victims in our midst: the politically excluded and the economically deprived, as well as those suffering from all manner of discrimination. The Easter dream of a beloved community based on equal fellowship with Christ enables us to detect social sin, the evil embedded in institutions and systems that oppress groups and individuals.

Resurrection faith also provides the perspective for understanding the saving mission of Christ. Karl Rahner rejects all notions that the death of Jesus appeased an angry God or paid off a debt owed to a demanding Deity. Throughout all of human history, God has offered participation in the divine life to all human beings, a self-communication that invites a loving response. Christians claim that Jesus of Nazareth, representing the whole human family, made a perfect response to this divine call by being totally obedient to the will of his Father, even unto death on the cross. As Rahner puts it: "We are saved because this man who is one of us has been saved by God and God has thereby made his salvific will present in the world historically, really and irrevocably."[3] This soteriology, or theology of salvation, puts the emphasis on God's ongoing and ultimately triumphant love for all human beings; on the perfect obedience of the man Jesus who is like us in all things but sin; and on the resurrection that vindicates the life and death of Jesus and plants the seeds of the final victory over sin. James Alison specifies this general approach by identifying Jesus as the innocent victim murdered by threatened leaders and as the scapegoat who breaks the usual cycle of responsive violence by forgiving all those complicit in his murder. In this way, the crucified and risen Christ forms a community of disciples based not on violence and vengeance but on compassion for victims and forgiveness of enemies.

An Easter faith that recognizes the fundamental goodness of human nature, the unconditional and triumphant love of God, and the self-sacrificing obedience of Christ challenges the popular understanding of original sin connected with the story of Adam and Eve, who enjoy a high

*state of perfection but disobey a law of God, incurring the divine wrath
and bringing guilt and suffering into the world.*

*In constructing a more contemporary account of original sin, Rahner
insists that we know original sin not from a reading of Genesis (the Jewish
community that produced this book has no doctrine of original sin) but
by reflecting on the human condition in the light of the resurrection.
Along the same line, the Protestant theologian Reinhold Niebuhr declared
that original sin is the one empirically verifiable Christian doctrine. The
world is not as God intended it: human communities fail to reflect the
ideals of the beloved community established by Christ, and individuals
fail to follow the law of love taught by Jesus.*

*According to Rahner, sin and guilt are universal and permanent and
therefore original. The human condition is flawed. All the sins committed
by human beings throughout history have produced a negative energy
in the world that is in conflict with the positive energy of God's grace.
As we make our earthly journey, we are influenced by both grace and sin,
by the good and bad example of others, by healthy institutions and unjust
systems, by the reign of God and the realm of evil. We know this from
our own experience, and we have good reason to assume that this is the
common experience of all human beings. Not only is this flawed state of
affairs universal, it is also permanent. The pool of evil formed by human
sins throughout history cannot be totally eradicated. Every utopian plan
that forgets this truth is doomed to failure. Temptations remain our lot
as we walk this earth. Rahner claims that only some form of free rejection
of God's self-giving love by the very primitive first humans can explain
the universal and permanent character of evil in the world. Alison suggests that this sin flowed from a form of acquisitive desire that was con-
trolled by instinct among animals but broke into violence among the first
humans when they realized they could try to acquire what the other
possessed.*

*The doctrine of original sin as interpreted by Rahner does not involve
a passing on of the first sin from generation to generation by propagation.
It does not destroy the fundamental goodness of human nature nor does
it incur the divine wrath. The first rejection of God's love did mar the
divine plan and introduce evil into the world. We now experience death
as dark and unknown. Our free choices are influenced by past sins of our
own and others. Sinful institutions and social structures perpetuate
injustice and oppression. Easter eyes, however, detect hints of divine grace*

stronger than all these effects of original sin. They recognize that salvation is open to all who follow the dictates of conscience and that unbaptized infants are in the hands of a loving God, who grants them the unmerited gift of eternal life.

Doctoral Studies

In 1971, my bishop assigned me to the campus ministry work that has occupied me ever since. In my first assignment at Bowling Green State University, I team-taught a course on Belief and Unbelief with a brilliant agnostic who had a broad knowledge of nineteenth- and twentieth-century intellectual history. It soon became evident to me that I needed a deeper grasp of contemporary theology in order to make a credible case for theism to collegians exposed to the modern critics of religion, including Ludwig Feuerbach, the father of modern atheism, and his skeptical descendants Marx, Nietzsche, Freud, and Sartre. I considered various great theologians as possible mentors for the ongoing engagement with the secular world demanded of a campus minister at a state university. The Lutheran theologian Paul Tillich was an intriguing possibility, since he presented Christian doctrines as answers to cultural questions and engaged in fruitful dialogue with important secular figures such as Einstein, Freud, and Picasso. Teilhard de Chardin was an interesting choice as well. He incorporated an evolutionary perspective and insights from modern science into his theological vision. As part of my search, I went to Munich for a visit with Karl Rahner in order to get a measure of the man behind the theology that had already enriched my ministry. After an intense conversation of an hour and twenty minutes with this energetic, brilliant man, I felt confident that studying his theology in greater depth was the best option for improving my ministry at a state university.

With the help of my bishop, who granted me a two-year study sabbatical, and John Macquarrie, the respected Anglican theologian who supervised my doctoral dissertation at the University of Oxford, I completed a study of Rahner's modern understanding of mystagogy that emphasized the need to elucidate the mystery dimension of contemporary experience as preparation for preaching the Christian message. It was later published under the title *Apologetics and the Eclipse of Mystery*, with an introduction by Rahner.

Personal Encounters

During those years of study, I spent a couple of months in Munich where I had the opportunity to interact personally with Rahner, a great blessing that helped me appreciate the spiritual and pastoral dimension of his work. He was a humble man, not really comfortable being the center of attention. With that in mind, I learned to resist the temptation to ask him theological questions during common meals. In our periodic private conversations, I was able to discuss theology and in the process learned more about him as a person: his volatile emotions, his ability to speak English (a fact not known to many others), his deep compassion, his anxiety about death, his interest in the ordinary things of life, his sober realism about the human condition, and his conviction that we are all immersed in the grace of the Holy Mystery. From others, I leaned of his admirable acts of private charity to the needy. Young Jesuits told me that when they drove him places, he would often urge them to go faster.

A number of personal encounters with Rahner rerun in my memory. I am in his room talking to him about his work and he shows me a large stack of typed pages. I ask if they are notes taken by his students, and he replies no, it is a draft of his new book *Grundkurs des Glaubens*, later translated as *Foundations of Christian Faith*. We take a walk together and stop in a coffeehouse. Rahner asks a lot of practical questions about how they prepare and serve the food. It is Holy Thursday, 1976, and I am in the chapel of the Jesuit residence in Munich, celebrating the Lord's Supper with about twenty of the residents. Rahner is sitting in the front row dressed in suit and tie. After the gospel he goes to the ambo, takes out a couple of typed pages, and reads his homily. He reminds us that the cross and the resurrection are joined together in the Eucharist and that the sacramental presence of Christ in the liturgy is the sign of his pneumatic presence in the everyday experiences of our lives. After developing this theme, he concludes with a reminder that the passion of the Lord recalled at Mass is to be lived in our daily lives. One day Rahner calls me to his room, shows me a dissertation written in English on his Christology, and asks me to write a critique of it (much later I learned—by accident—that he incorporated my whole evaluation in a letter to the author). Once again, we are in his room with an Irish seminarian who is taking dictation. Rahner is pacing the floor composing an introduction to my book *Apologetics and the Eclipse of Mystery* and trying to do it in English. The whole thing is not going well, and I finally convince him to do it in German and we will translate it later. Rahner continues to pace, like a caged tiger, and completes the introduction. At one point, I suggest it sounds arrogant to say "the only criticism I take very seriously" comes from my student and friend Johann Metz. He replies that this is exactly what he means and he is not changing it. These and other personal interactions with Rahner are for me treasured moments of grace that gave me a deeper appreciation of the man and his theology.

Reflection on the Priesthood

In 2000, I was asked by the National Federation of Priests' Councils to participate in a dialogue titled "Styles and Models of Priestly Ministry." I represented the position of Karl Rahner. Robert Barron, then a professor at Mundelein seminary, presented the position of Hans Urs von Balthasar. Prompted by questions from the moderator Peter Feldmeier, I spoke of my personal relationship with Rahner, offered an overview of his theology, commented on his Ignatian-based spirituality, and tried to respond to Barron's well-articulated criticisms of Rahner from a Balthasarian perspective. As the conversation focused more on the priesthood, I noted that Rahner emphasized the prophetic role of priests, which highlights proclaiming the Word in various ways and settings. There is a Rahnerian style of preaching that relates the Scripture readings to the real-life concerns of people today. I shared my concern that priests educated primarily on Balthasar's theology will find it difficult to make realistic applications to pastoral concerns. Surely, creative theologians like Bob Barron and other gifted priests can do this. My fear is that many other priests will not be able to make good pastoral use of Balthasar's theology. While Rahner helps the pastoral task by suggesting connections with the lived experience of people today, Balthasar rejects the correlational method in favor of simply presenting the Christian message in all its beauty. Personally, I love to read Balthasar. He was one of the great minds of the twentieth century, with a remarkable grasp of the rich Christian tradition. He had an uncanny ability to reveal the inner dynamic of other thinkers. His essays on various writers such as Origen, Bonaventure, Dante, and Hopkins are masterful. But after reading them, I am hard pressed to know how to use what I learned in my pastoral work. For this reason I want to keep the Rahnerian method of correlation as an essential part of seminary education and pastoral practice.

In response to a question about how I do priestly ministry from a Rahnerian viewpoint, I replied that his theology provides a perspective and framework for everything I do as a priest. When I am faithful to the ideals Rahner embodied and taught, I feel integrated and energized. Fidelity to his wisdom moves me to seek guidance from many sources, including Balthasar, the liberationists, the neoconservatives, and secular sources. For me, however, most of this input gets filtered into a Rahnerian framework. He reminds me to accept my limitations and to rely on the Gracious Mystery. He prods me to treat others with respect and to be open to receiving love and knowledge from those I serve. His theology moves me to be on alert for clues to the presence of the Spirit in the lives of all who cross my path.

Rahner's theology raises up Christ as the model for servant-leadership in the community of faith and in the academic world where I minister. He helps me deal with the heavy demands of priesthood by reminding me that no one is required to do the impossible and that my task is to empower others. His emphasis on the priest as proclaimer of the Word is a constant reminder of the need to prepare well for preaching at the Eucharist. His mystagogical method demands good, descriptive material in homilies that opens up the mystery dimension of life and prepares for hearing the Gospel message. He reminds me not to offer glib answers to people suffering deeply or grieving the loss of a loved one. His call is to face life in all its harsh reality with trust in the God who brings all things to completion. I resonate with this sober realism. When I repeatedly fail to live up to all those ideals, Rahner points me to Jesus who lived and spoke God's forgiveness. I have taken my comments out of the context of the dialogue with Robert Barron in order to highlight Rahner's great influence on me personally.

Sex Abuse Scandal

Not long after the sex abuse scandal became national news in 2002, Renew International, a Catholic organization devoted to spiritual renewal, asked me to offer some workshops for priests trying to make sense of this horrendous story. In preparation, I spent some time listening to victims and to priests who expressed a wide variety of responses. Rahner's sober realism prompted me to face the full horror of the situation. His paschal theology alerted me to signs of hope in this dark tragedy. I summarized some of my findings and thoughts in the following 2003 article.

Perspectives on the Sex Abuse Scandal

In January 2002, the priest sex abuse issue, which had received periodic media attention since 1985, burst into the national spotlight when the Boston Globe *began a series of reports charging that a former Boston priest had molested more than 130 young boys while being moved from parish to parish by archdiocesan officials. Throughout the year, the scandal grew as more allegations of abuse and negligence were made public, creating an unprecedented crisis for the whole American church. My own impressions of the scandal are influenced not only by media reports but also by conversations with some brave victims and with numerous priests from around the country.*

The vast majority of the 46,000 priests in the United States have not abused children. All of us, however, are deeply affected by the abhorrent acts of a few (less than 1 percent, according to commonly cited statistics) of our brothers in ministry. Priests are uniformly sad over the suffering of the abused children and teenagers. Some priests, however, are so distressed over the whole issue that they tend to avoid facing it directly. Others have listened to the heartrending stories of victims and found themselves more empathetic to their plight. They recognize that abuse by a priest affects young victims at a deep level because the clergy represent for them God and the church. Some victims are scarred for life. They need spiritual healing as well as therapy. From church leaders, they want not only apologies but also assurances that the abuse was not their fault and that they have actually served the interests of the church by coming forward to speak about their traumatic experiences. Priests who respond to the cries of the victims perform an important service and are in a better position to preach the Gospel message of forgiveness.

Priests, like everyone else touched by this scandal, recognize the importance of uncovering the underlying causes. A few of the perpetrators are clearly pedophiles who are sexually attracted to prepubescent children. There are great doubts about the power of therapy to change their orientation, and these men must be excluded from ministry in order to protect children. Authors have offered various explanations for this horrible abuse of minors. In his book The Courage to Be Catholic, *George Weigel locates the problem in a lack of fidelity to priestly ideals fostered by the laxity, dissent, and soft leadership prevalent in the church since Vatican II. His solution includes a greater emphasis on the unique identity of the priest as another Christ and on fidelity to official church teaching and discipline. Some Vatican officials, aware that most of the victims are teenage boys, blame the crisis on the large number of homosexual men in the priesthood who espouse or accept a promiscuous gay culture. One radical response, said to be under consideration in Rome, is to bar all homosexual men from ordination. The popular spiritual writer Richard Rohr points out that mandatory celibacy not only limits the pool of candidates for the priesthood but also traps men who are committed to ordained ministry in a lifestyle they did not really want and cannot successfully manage. Rohr wants celibacy to be a part of an intense preparation for ministry followed by the option to marry. Bishop Thomas Gumbleton argues that the problem is not gays in the priesthood or mandatory celibacy but the arrested psycho-sexual development of some priests who act out with minors. An effective solution must include better seminary training and personal counseling to foster healthy sexual development. Noting that over 90 percent of applicants are accepted into seminaries, Donald Cozzens, author of the groundbreaking book* The Changing Face of the Priesthood, *calls for better screening methods designed to detect potential problems ahead of time. Convinced that the all-male clerical culture fosters immaturity, Joan Chittister and other feminists insist on a radically restructured priesthood open to women. Some of these expla-*

nations overlap, and none appears totally comprehensive and compelling. The good of the church demands a thorough and honest study of the root causes of the problem.

   Priests generally feel a strong sense of compassion for their brothers who have been removed from ministry. All of us know personally someone charged with abusing minors. These men need understanding and support. Many of them have lived virtuous lives in other ways and have done fine ministerial work. Their failures in one area of life, no matter how harmful, do not make them evil persons or vitiate all the good they have done. Most priests hesitate to cast stones at their erring brothers. They know too much about the demands of ordained ministry and the challenges of living a celibate life to be harsh on others. All of us priests are guilty, in one way or the other, of tarnishing the high ideals of the priesthood. The good news is that Jesus gave forgiveness and conversion such a prominent place in his teaching. The treatment of guilty priests should be governed by the Gospel and not media pressure or the advice of lawyers. Zero tolerance does not reflect Gospel values. Obviously, some erring priests have to be excluded from ministry, but there are others who deserve another chance and pose no reasonable threat to minors.

   The scandal has generated a good deal of anger and resentment among priests. The American bishops as a whole are a favorite target for a variety of reasons: for caving in to the media and adopting the unfair zero tolerance policy; for making priests the scapegoats and failing to call to account their negligent brother bishops; for breaking the traditional bond of trust with their priests; for ignoring the priest shortage problem; for caring more about protecting the institution and their own reputations than about people who need help; and for kowtowing to the Roman Curia that treats them more like subordinates than successors of the apostles. The media also ignites clerical anger for overplaying the scandal, for demonstrating a lingering anti-Catholic bias, for emphasizing the sensational, and for failing to report positive progress on the issue.

   Priests today give voice to a new set of fears: A disgruntled parishioner could make a false accusation or blow an innocent sign of affection out of proportion and ruin my reputation. People are more reserved around me and less likely to share their deeper concerns. I don't feel comfortable wearing clericals in public. People working in the hospital look away or ignore me when I make my rounds visiting the sick. Some of my parishioners, upset with the bishops, might reduce their support and participation in the parish. *Some fears get expressed as open-ended questions that reflect a deeper anxiety. Is there ever going to be an end to this mess? What will the church look like on the other side of this crisis? What does the scandal mean in the long run? What fundamental changes will there be in the priesthood? Where is God in these horrible events?*

During this past year, the Los Angeles Times *took an extensive opinion survey of priests throughout the country. Remarkably, they found that in the midst of the scandal, 70 percent of the priests in the United States are very satisfied with the way their lives as priests are going. About 21 percent are somewhat satisfied, and only 6 percent are very or somewhat dissatisfied. This confirms my own impression that priests preserve their mental health by distinguishing the larger problems in the church as a whole, which are extremely distressing, from their day-to-day ministry, which brings them a sense of fulfillment and satisfaction. By concentrating on serving others and meeting their ministerial responsibilities, priests are able to maintain a fundamentally positive outlook, which includes the conviction that the church will emerge strengthened and healthier in the long run because of the scandal.*

Many laypeople, who have their own distinct responses to the scandal, share the sadness, anger, fears, and questions of priests as we struggle together to maintain hope in the midst of the current crisis. In contrast to optimism, which is rooted in human achievement, Christian hope is based on the power of God to bring good out of evil. Our God is totally trustworthy and will never abandon us or the church. Despite our sins and failures, the fundamental energy of the universe flows toward integrity and fulfillment. Jesus Christ is the concrete embodiment of divine fidelity, and his resurrection unleashed the full power of the Spirit, who remains with the church, enabling it to survive scandals including this unprecedented crisis. We remain people of hope because we are united to Christ who fulfills the divine promises and sends the Spirit to guide us.

This faith conviction alerts us to signals of hope in the midst of the current crisis. Hundreds of victims have come forward and have begun a healing process, which is healthy for them and the church. Some priests, shorn of automatic respect, have become more empathetic to those on the margins, more committed to genuine servant-leadership, and more reliant on the power of prayer. Laypeople have formed associations seeking greater involvement in the life of the church. Priests and laity are meeting in small groups to discuss and pray for healing of the Body of Christ. Around the country, there have been very few reported cases of abuse during the last decade—a remarkable development that deserves more attention and study. All such signs of hope remind us that God can indeed bring good out of this heartrending scandal.

A decade since I wrote that article, the church is still suffering from the scandal. Periodically, new allegations surface, but not as many as before. Some dioceses have released records and become more transparent, while others have been less forthcoming. We understand pedophilia better. Catholics remain angry at bishops who have not taken responsibility for their part in the abuse of minors. The screening of seminary candidates has improved. There are still disagreements on fundamental causes and long-term solutions. The church has not expanded the pool of candidates to the priesthood, although some comments by Pope Francis have given new hope for exceptions to mandatory celibacy. We still need prayers for healing, forgiveness, and wisdom in moving forward.

Ministering to Collegians

Influenced by Rahner, I have tried to better understand the collegians I served for over five decades. Here is one of my efforts to pull together some of what I learned.

The Spirituality of Catholic Collegians

What are today's Catholic college students really like? The question has broad significance because Catholics constitute over 30 percent of the collegiate population, and they will join other young adults in shaping the future of our society. The Catholic community has a special interest in the spirituality of these students as we contemplate the future of a church in an unprecedented crisis.

Students in college at the beginning of the new millennium are on a spiritual journey very similar to their parents. They have the same spiritual longings as previous generations for meaning and purpose in life.

These millennials, as they are sometimes called, have to contend with the essential conflict between their infinite longings and their finite capabilities. They know the age-old struggle between grace and sin. Their challenges sound familiar: forming their personal identity, developing good friendships, finding a life partner, choosing a career, appropriating their religious heritage, cultivating habits of good citizenship, and deciding how to relate to the dominant culture. Fads in music, dress, dance, and language change rapidly, but human nature remains common. Millennials still fall in love, treasure friends, and empathize with suffering loved ones.

American culture continues to exercise great influence on millennial collegians, often at a preconscious level. Some cultural trends, such as rugged individualism, unbridled hedonism, lavish consumerism, and uncritical nationalism, are anti-Gospel and harmful to their spiritual growth. Other ideals, including authenticity, self-actualization, freedom, and volunteerism, when placed in a Christian framework, can promote healthy spiritual development. Collegians grow up in a country where over 90 percent of the citizens say they believe in God and pray periodically, and over 60 percent are affiliated with a religious organization. During the last four years of the twentieth century, polls indicated that interest in spirituality among teenagers increased almost 25 percent, a trend that anecdotal evidence suggests is continuing. Collegians reflect the ambivalent mix of secular and religious currents in our culture.

For the most part, the richly textured Catholic subculture that shaped Catholic spirituality in the past has disappeared. Catholic millennials have grown up with greater religious pluralism than their grandparents. Most of them have not known an integrated Catholic world that transmits a coherent vision of the faith. They have, rather, gleaned fragments of their spirituality from various sources, including their families, parish liturgies, youth retreats, religious education classes, and for some, Catholic schools. This process has produced collegians with greater tolerance but less institutional loyalty than previous generations of Catholics.

Recent sociological studies of young adults indicate that most Catholic collegians today maintain certain fundamental beliefs that can help ground a viable spirituality. Around 90 percent affirm the divinity of Christ and believe that at Mass the bread and wine become his Body and Blood. They consider helping the poor as important to their faith as believing in the real presence of Christ in the Eucharist. Although most Catholic collegians have no explicit working knowledge of the Second Vatican Council, many have appropriated (presumably from diverse ecclesial and cultural sources) important conciliar themes. Foremost is the crucial conviction that we are the church, which means practically that the faithful should have a voice in how parishes are run. These millenials also demonstrate an incipient understanding of the communal nature of the liturgy, the importance of religious liberty, the value of ecumenical and interfaith dialogue, the expanded role of laity in the church, the unique mediatorship of Christ, and the need to work for social justice. My students often find that formal study of these conciliar teachings affirms general perceptions they already hold.

Although Catholic millennials share certain common characteristics, their spiritual passions and interests are quite diverse. We can examine this pluralism by distinguishing seven types of spirituality: eclipsed, private, ecumenical, evangelical, sacramental, prophetic, and communal.

Eclipsed: A good number of Catholic collegians show no particular interest in religious or spiritual matters. They do not attend Mass on campus and seldom pray. Some feel they are too busy or have higher priorities, while others experience guilt feelings that blunt their spiritual longings. Yet they remain religious beings and identify themselves as Catholics in surveys. Their spirituality is not destroyed but rather eclipsed by their current concerns. We can hope that the ordinary process of maturation or some major event, such as a personal crisis, the death of a loved one, getting married, or having a baby, will uncover their latent spiritual needs.

Private: Some Catholic collegians seldom attend liturgies or participate in church activities but pursue spiritual goals in other ways: for example, reading religious books, communing with nature, and praying privately. Their private spiritual journey can be fulfilling, but, unconnected to traditional wisdom, it is threatened by fads and superficiality. Our hope is that they will discover and tap into the rich spiritual tradition of their Catholic heritage.

Ecumenical: A growing number of millennials simply assume that the divisions among Christians make no sense, and that we all should unite and work together. Some are loyal to their Catholic heritage, but others have little institutional loyalty and would join another Christian denomination if it brought them closer to Christ and better served their spiritual needs. In this competitive situation, we need vibrant Catholic parishes that will utilize the gifts and meet the needs of today's collegians.

Evangelical: *A growing number of Catholic collegians manifest an evangelical piety. They speak easily about their personal relationship to Jesus and gravitate to prayer groups with high emotional energy. They resonate with some of the themes of the new evangelization, including the effort to share their faith with others. Some are charismatic in orientation, emphasizing the gifts of the Holy Spirit. A few are truly fundamentalists who act aggressively in preserving their Catholic heritage from the threats of the contemporary world and the reforms of Vatican II, which appear to them as excessive and dangerous. The church on campus should welcome the evangelical Catholics and learn how to tap their energy and enthusiasm.*

Sacramental: *Many Catholic millennials still love their church and find their spiritual nourishment through fairly regular participation in the official liturgy and traditional practices. As a result, they are attuned to the presence of God in everyday life and have a general sense of the sacramental character of the whole world. Some of them report mystical experiences, while others simply trust that God is present in their daily lives. These students often need affirmation that their spiritual intuitions are in accord with the core spirituality of the Catholic tradition.*

Prophetic: *Most campus ministry programs have a small group of students committed to working in various ways for justice and peace in the world. They align themselves with the goals of organizations like Pax Christi and Bread for the World, devote themselves to causes such as racial harmony and environmental health, and try to help those in need. The developing tradition of Catholic social thought can be a great source of guidance and inspiration for them.*

Communal: *Many millennial Catholics feel the need to associate with others who share their values. They like worshiping with kindred spirits at Mass, using their gifts for the benefit of the church, and participating in faith-sharing groups. They often need reminders that an authentic communal spirituality maintains dialogue with the larger world.*

The older categories of conservative and liberal, based on responses to Vatican II, are no longer adequate to describe the millennials, who have no experience and little knowledge of the council. They have a new set of challenges and diverse ways of relating to the Catholic tradition, but they are empowered by the same Spirit, who is the real basis of our hope for this generation of collegians.

Spiritual Direction

Rahner's theological anthropology has been a major influence on my ministry as a spiritual guide. I have listened to persons tell their stories conscious that they are self-transcendent beings, oriented to mystery. The people who come to see me are all a mixture of infinite longings and finite capabilities. We both know ourselves as a question for whom there is no definitive answer on this earth. Rahner's dialectical anthropology alerts me to specific tensions individuals experience between competing tendencies. For example, the tension between the desire for a love imperishable and the limitations of all love relationships.

My ear is attuned to extreme reactions to the common challenges of life that require virtuous responses: for example, a mindless relativism or a constricted exclusivism that needs the virtue of committed openness; a naïve optimism or a cynical pessimism that requires the virtue of hopeful-realism; a paralyzing introspection or an unexamined frenzy that calls for reflective-spontaneity; and a childish outlook or a pseudosophistication that demands enlightened-simplicity. I often suggest to people that they use these dialectical virtues for a systematic self-examination as a springboard to spiritual growth. A pastoral minister, for example, can ask herself if she is really committed to the long and rich Catholic tradition or only selective parts of it. A parish council member can ask himself if he is truly open to the ideas and initiatives of all the parishioners or only a few favorites. A father can discover that he is overly optimistic in assessing the academic potential of his children. A woman deeply committed to a professional career may discern that she is living a frenzied life and needs more time for prayerful reflection. An examination of conscience based on dialectical virtues reveals our strengths and suggests areas for improvement.

In directing individuals who complain of a lack of consolation in their prayer life, I suggest they read an article I wrote on Mother Teresa.

Mother Teresa's Dark Night of the Soul

Years after the death of Mother Teresa in 1997, we are now able to relate the well-known story of her admirable life of service to the remarkable, mostly-hidden story of her interior spiritual life. The publication of Mother Teresa: Come Be My Light, *edited with commentary by Fr. Brian Kolodiejchuk, the advocate for her canonization, has made public many private letters that the "Saint of Calcutta" wrote to various spiritual confidants. They reveal her protracted struggle with an agonizing interior darkness, what* Time *magazine called "a beloved icon's fifty-year crisis of faith."*

Mother Teresa's dark night of the soul is even more striking when compared with her previous comforting experiences of an intimate relationship with Christ. "From childhood the Heart of Jesus has been my first love,"[4] she recalled in a letter to one of her spiritual confidants, and added in a subsequent letter: "From the age of 5 1/2 years—when I first received Him [in Holy Communion]—the love for souls has been within."[5] By the age of twelve, she knew she wanted to be a missionary to the poor. When she was eighteen, she left a very happy home life to join the Sisters of Our Lady of Loreto. Forty years later she wrote: "I've never doubted even for a second that I've done the right thing; it was the will of God. It was His choice."[6]

The future "Saint of Calcutta" made her final vows as a Sister of Loreto on May 24, 1937. In a letter to a priest in her hometown, she expressed some of her deeper feelings on the occasion: "How happy I was that I could, of my own free will, ignite my own sacrifice."[7] She now saw herself as "the spouse of Jesus" and declared, "I would give everything, even life itself, for Him."[8] She carried out her spousal commitment by teaching at St. Mary's High School in Calcutta and later serving as principal. Her desire for closer union with God drove her in April 1942 to make a secret private vow to God binding herself under pain of mortal sin "to give to God anything that He may ask, 'Not to refuse Him anything.' "[9] This secret vow, rooted in her total trust of God's unconditional love, gave her a great sense of inner joy and a cheerful spirit in serving others.

On September 10, 1946, Mother Teresa was traveling by train to a retreat site when Christ called her "to go out in the streets to serve the poorest of the poor." It was "a call within a call" to "satiate the thirst of Jesus,"[10] a reference to his cry on the cross, "I thirst," interpreted as an infinite thirst for love and souls. During the next ten months, Mother Teresa had many intimate conversations with Jesus, who addressed her as "my own spouse" pleading with her: "Come, come carry Me into the holes of the poor. Come, be My Light." [11] *Jesus often punctuated the plea by asking, "Wilt thou refuse?" Not only did she hear the voice of the Lord, she also had vivid visions. In the most significant one, she is a little child standing with Mary facing Jesus on the cross. She sees a great crowd of children and poor people covered in darkness and Jesus says, "Will you refuse to do this for Me, to take care of them to bring them to Me?" She answers, "You know, Jesus, I am ready to go at a minute's notice."* [12]

In August of 1948, Mother Teresa finally received permission from Rome to leave the Loreto sisters and respond to the call she was sure came from the Lord. Thus began her ministry to the poorest of the poor. Her story became familiar to the world: the demanding daily routine of prayer and selfless service to the homeless in Calcutta; the founding of the Missionaries of Charity that eventually had houses in over one hundred countries; the worldwide renown, including the Nobel Peace Prize; the state funeral from the Indian government televised to millions around the world.

From the time she embarked on her "call within a call," Mother Teresa's inner life took a dramatic, wrenching turn. She no longer heard the voice of "her spouse," or experienced any more visions. The comforting warmth of her relationship to Jesus turned to ice. Over the course of five decades, she periodically tried to describe her interior darkness to various spiritual directors. She wrote of feeling alone, unwanted, forsaken. When she tried to raise her thoughts to heaven, "there is such convicting emptiness that those very thoughts return like sharp knives and hurt my very soul. . . . I am told God loves me and yet the reality of darkness and coldness and emptiness is so great that nothing touches my soul." [13] *People who encounter her joyful spirit think that intimacy with God absorbs her heart, but really "cheerfulness is the cloak by which I cover the emptiness and misery."* [14] *She suffered from "pains without ceasing" and "untold agony" and was afraid to uncover the "many unanswered questions" that "live within me."* [15]

The darkness and emptiness were horrible, but even worse is the pain of her intense longing for God. The tremendous contradiction between her desire for God and God's absence is so sharp that she fears that it "will unbalance me." She worries about being hypocritical since she speaks to others about the "tender love of God" and yet "no light or inspiration enters my soul," leaving her with the "terrible pain of loss—of God not wanting me."[16]

In 1961, one of her more astute spiritual directors, Fr. Joseph Neuner, advised her that "the only response to this trial is the total surrender to God and the acceptance of the darkness in union with Jesus." She took his advice and reported that for the first time in eleven years she came "to love the darkness" and this brought her "a deep joy." Although the darkness continued to assail her the rest of her life (with one five-week respite after the death of Pope Pius XII in 1958), she accepted it and was able to carry on her ministry to the poor with a cheerful spirit and a radiant smile on her face.

How are we to understand Mother Teresa's portrayal of her inner spiritual life? All religious experiences are personally and culturally conditioned. Throughout Christian history, saints have described their encounters with the ultimately mysterious God in words, images, and categories familiar to them. Since Mother Teresa thought of her relationship to Jesus in spousal terms, it is not surprising that she heard Jesus address her as "my spouse." Her tremendous capacity for self-giving love disposed her to interpret God's love for her as an ever greater call to self-sacrifice. Her own natural instinct to help one poor person at a time may explain why she heard no divine call to challenge the unjust structures and systems that imprison so many in poverty. Her passionate desire to love Jesus more than he has ever been loved sets the stage for his oft-repeated question to her, "Wilt thou refuse me?" Because she saw Christ in the Eucharist, she could see the poor as Christ in disguise.

When Mother Teresa writes with great anguish about Jesus still suffering today because poor persons and little children are not being saved, we can recognize her own theological outlook rather than assume this is a divinely revealed truth. Suggestions that God was testing her love with those horrible spiritual torments is likewise theologically questionable. Perhaps her dark night was rooted in her tremendous capacity for empathy. She had a profound sympathy for the crucified Christ who felt abandoned by God. She often spoke of the great suffering of the poor who were left alone and unloved. We can imagine her deep identification with Christ and the poor predisposing her to participate spiritually in their sense of abandonment. She herself wrote: "The physical situation of my poor left in the streets unwanted, unloved, unclaimed are the true picture of my own spiritual life." Whatever the mysterious dynamic of her interior suffering, the truly remarkable fact, both instructive and inspiring, is

> that *Mother Teresa carried on her mission to the poorest of the poor for half a century without spiritual consolation but always with "a hearty 'yes' to God and a big smile for all."* [17]

In doing spiritual direction, I find it useful to recall elements of Rahner's spiritual journey. A man trying to be more open to his emotional life finds encouragement in Rahner's growing emphasis on love and personal relationships as the place where people today find clues to the Holy Mystery. To a woman seeking a closer relationship to Christ, I describe the development in Rahner's own relationship to Jesus Christ. As a young man he was more attracted to the Christ presented by Paul than to the Jesus portrayed in the Synoptic Gospels. I tell her about Rahner only gradually becoming comfortable with throwing his arms around Jesus in an act of love, and, taken with this image, she finds new energy for her own spiritual quest. Many serious searchers like this woman find comfort and inspiration in the fact that a great theologian like Rahner grew only gradually to greater maturity in his relationship to Jesus. Rahner reminds all of us that Christianity is not an abstract ideal but involves a developing relationship to a historical person, the Word made flesh, who walked this earth and shared our joys and sufferings.

Preaching

Throughout my whole priesthood, Rahner has been especially helpful in meeting the primary pastoral responsibility of proclaiming the Word. Early in my ministry, his collections of sermons (*Biblical Homilies* and *The Eternal Year*) provided valuable perspectives on the Scripture readings for Sundays and holy days. Over the years, I came to a greater understanding of his whole approach to preparing homilies that I now use automatically.

A number of years ago I wrote a book, along with my psychologist friend Kevin Anderson, titled *A Light Unto My Path: Crafting Effective Homilies* (Paulist 2006) that develops this Rahnerian approach to preaching. I continue to think it can be a valuable guide for those charged with the preaching ministry. The book's main point is drawn from Rahner's method of correlation that calls for a mutually critical dialogue between the normative Christian tradition and the contemporary world, with its deep concerns and complex mixture of grace and sin. Based on this method, the book suggests that preachers preparing homilies set up a conversation between the assigned Scripture texts and the existential concerns of the congregation. This can be done through both personal reflection and actual discussions with individuals and groups. The important point is to find a focus for the homily that relates the personal interests, concerns, and challenges of the congregation with the essential teaching found in the readings. For example, a homily on Mark 4:35-41 (Jesus calms the storm after his fearful disciples call for help) would describe the fears and anxieties experienced by various members of the congregation and show that Jesus, by word and example, teaches that trust in God is the great antidote to the unavoidable fears of life. This approach is fundamentally different from the thematic method proposed in many preaching guides that elucidate a theme found in the Sunday readings. The problem with that approach is that even a well-developed theme may have no relevance for this particular congregation.

Through our national scientific survey, Kevin Anderson and I discovered that people commonly criticize sermons for being "back there," in the biblical period, or "up there," out of touch with their current experience. On the other hand, one of the great predictors of perceived homily effectiveness is the following statement: the preacher understands my heart. Finding a proper focus for a homily that makes a connection between real existential concerns and Christian wisdom makes it far more likely that hearers of the Word will be touched in heart and mind. Highly talented preachers will find their own creative ways to proclaim the Word effectively. I am convinced, however, that other preachers can be far more effective by following the Rahnerian approach of developing a specific focus point for each homily, as illustrated in the following.

Labor Day and a Spirituality of Work

On this Labor Day weekend, which represents the end of summer leisure and the return to a more demanding work schedule, we have the opportunity to reflect on the role work plays in our lives. Work includes all purposeful human activity including earning a living, doing our job, raising children, as well as volunteering to serve others and the common good. We all should be aware that some of us gathered here have been looking for a job for months without any success, while others have tedious jobs that do not pay a living wage. Among those who are employed and well paid there is the temptation to make an idol out of work, to assign a higher priority to the job than the family or even God. We have growing numbers of people who identify themselves as workaholics. Many Americans are overworked, spending more time at the job than workers in other industrialized countries. As a lot of people here know firsthand, the more successful individuals are at their job, the more hours they put in.

It is difficult for all of us to handle all the temptations associated with work: the underemployed woman who has lost her sense of self-esteem and is consumed by anger at God; the corporate executive who is feeling guilty for stepping on people climbing the corporate ladder; the mother who identified herself with raising children and is now overwhelmed by the empty nest syndrome; the workaholic who neglects her family responsibilities; the professor who is envious of the scholarly accomplishments of her colleagues; the student who is hurting her health by working an extra job; a man who considers himself a failure because he earns less money than his friends. It is not easy to keep our work in proper perspective. Let us take a couple minutes to reflect silently on any ways our work is keeping us from being better Christian disciples.

Today's gospel is from chapter 14 of Luke. We can hear it as a call to keep our priorities straight. Following Christ involves hating parents and children and siblings. Even allowing for Semitic hyperbole, the message is radical and clear: Nothing in life is as important as following Christ. Doing God's will is even more important than attending to family relationships or any other human activity, including work. Discipleship is about keeping priorities in order. Jesus goes on to tell us that following him involves the cross. We can't be good disciples without taking up the crosses connected with work. We can hear the example of building a tower or preparing for battle as a reminder that we have to use our heads in meeting the challenges of life including our work situation. Prudence is an important virtue. Strategy and calculation play a necessary role in human affairs.

As we relate this advice of Jesus to the challenges of work, we should remember that he was a worker himself, a carpenter. As a Galilean peasant under Roman rule, we can be sure he was undercompensated. As an ordinary citizen of Nazareth, we can presume he was a hard worker, did his job well, and helped support his family.

There is a proper spirituality of work based on the Gospel. The task of spreading the kingdom deserves our best efforts. A more reliable measure of our success in life is our contribution to the common good. The teachings of Jesus establish a framework for reflecting on a proper ordering of priorities. Perhaps we could think of work as the way we actualize ourselves, and in the process become a better family member. Work is the way we cooperate with God in spreading the kingdom in the family and in the world. For disciples of Christ, work bears all these deeper meanings. Our work should not define us, but it is a gift that enables us to grow spiritually and to make the world a better place.

This faith perspective can help all of us manage better the temptations surrounding work. A woman discouraged by her job situation may find new energy to prepare herself for a better job. An executive decides to treat her work colleagues with greater respect. A mother expands her interests, preparing for the day her children leave home. A workaholic resolves to spend more time with his family. A teacher becomes less competitive and more satisfied with the important work he does. A student cuts back on her work hours, spends less money, and devotes more time to study. Let us take a minute of silence to reflect on Jesus the worker and any specific ways he is calling us to develop a deeper spirituality of work.

Liturgical Year

Parish life is punctuated by the rhythm of the liturgical year. The reflective mood established by the four Sundays of Advent prepares us for the joyful celebration of the birth of Jesus and the Christmas season that extends to the baptism of the Lord. The forty days of Lent prepare for the jubilant celebration of the resurrection of Christ and the fifty-day Easter season that invites continuing reflection on the meaning of the resurrection. In between, we celebrate Ordinary Time, which has its own message for our daily lives. Christmas and Easter are always the high points of parish celebrations. They draw the largest crowds and require the most time and energy by way of preparation. Rahner's *The Great Church Year*, which contains homilies and meditations that follow the liturgical cycle, has proven a valuable resource for me in preparing homilies for Sunday liturgies and holy-day feasts. Each time I reread the material, I find some new insight that escaped me before. Often something Rahner wrote will send me to other authors for further clarification and development. It has always seemed important to respond positively to the larger crowds on Christmas and Easter. Rather than berate people for not showing up regularly for Mass, wise presiders make them feel welcome and do their best job of preaching a meaningful homily that might entice them to attend more often. For many years, I have tried to enhance the celebration of Christmas and Easter by writing an article that people could use for further reflection on the incarnation and resurrection.

Christmas: Celebrating the Power of Jesus

The traditional nativity scene, depicting Mary and Joseph hovering protectively over the baby Jesus in the manger, can bring back nostalgic childhood memories and evoke warm sentimental feelings. At the same time, the presence of the shepherds and the Magi in the scene invites us to a more mature and sober consideration of the remarkable angelic proclamation that this baby is really the Savior who is Christ the Lord, destined to be a powerful ruler. Thus, the traditional nativity scene that recalls a childlike sense of serene security also prompts serious reflection on the challenging claim that Jesus is the Savior of all, the definitive Prophet, the most powerful figure in human history.

Reflecting on the power of Jesus takes us back to the great Hebrew prophets who proclaimed the coming of a mighty Messiah. Isaiah, to take just one example, spoke of a God-Hero who would smash the rod of the taskmaster; a Wonder-Counselor who would provide a great light for those dwelling in the land of gloom; a Prince of Peace who would exercise a dominion vast and forever peaceful (Isa 9:1-6). In due time, the prophecies were fulfilled when the Holy Spirit overshadowed Mary of Nazareth, and the almighty Word of God took flesh and pitched his tent in our midst. The long-awaited Messiah was from the beginning protected by almighty God. As Matthew tells the story, a greatly troubled King Herod sought to destroy Jesus after he heard from the Magi about a "newborn king of the Jews." The evil intentions of this power hungry king were thwarted because a Higher Power sent a message in a dream to Joseph to flee with Mary and Jesus to Egypt. They remained there until Herod died and then made their way back to Nazareth, a safer place where Jesus grew to manhood, his power hidden in the everyday routine of a Galilean peasant who followed his father's trade as a carpenter.

In his early thirties, Jesus left Nazareth and traveled south to Bethany in Judea, where he was baptized by John, who was preaching a baptism of repentance for sin. All four gospels note that on this occasion the Spirit came down upon Jesus in the form of a dove, remaining with him throughout his public life as the source of his amazing power. The Spirit, for instance, led Jesus out into the desert where he entered into fierce spiritual combat with Satan. Despite his weakened physical condition after a forty-day fast, he resisted Satan's efforts to subvert his mission. Three times, Jesus refused to take the easy way out and remained faithful to the will of his Father. At the end of the ordeal, Luke suggests that Satan would look for future opportunities to test Jesus, but this initial encounter established the essential point: Jesus is more powerful than all the demonic forces.

Empowered by the Spirit and fresh from his victorious encounter with Satan, Jesus took up his mission to establish the reign of God in the world and to bring salvation to all people. As Mark's gospel makes clear, he continued to demonstrate his power over demons by frequent exorcisms during his public ministry (1:39). The unclean spirits recognized that he was the Holy One of God and that he had the power to destroy them (1:24). So great was the power of Jesus over demons that he could share it with his disciples as he sent them forth on a mission of preaching and exorcising (3:15).

The followers of Jesus came to know him as a man commended by God who performed "mighty deeds, signs, and wonders" (Acts 2:22). In the gospels, Jesus performs a great variety of mighty deeds that demonstrate his mastery over nature and his ability to cure diseases. These miracles are signs of the presence of God's reign in the world, but they also manifest his personal power. Consider the story of the woman afflicted with hemorrhages for twelve years who is cured simply by touching the tassel on the cloak of Jesus (Luke 8:40-48). This intriguing detail suggests that Jesus possessed an energy source or healing power so strong and available that it could be tapped even apart from a conscious decision on his part to utilize it. In most healings, however, Jesus consciously shares his power with those seeking help. Sometimes, he effects a cure instantly and even at a distance, as in the cure of the daughter of the persistent and clever

Canaanite woman (Matt 15:21-28). In other situations, Jesus employs a more hands-on approach, as when he cures the man born blind by spitting on the ground, making clay, smearing it on his eyes, and having him wash in the Pool of Siloam (John 9:1-8). Allowing for various methods, the gospels insist that both friends and foes recognized the remarkable power of Jesus to cure diseases of all kinds.

The disciples were also awestruck by the power of Jesus over nature. When he calmed the violent squall that terrified the disciples in a boat on the sea, they were "filled with great awe" and asked: "Who then is this whom even wind and sea obey?" (Mark 4:35-41). The story of the feeding of the multitudes is recounted six times in the gospels, suggesting the great significance this mighty deed had for the early church in extolling the nourishing power of Christ. When Jesus walked on the sea and the wind died down, the disciples were "completely astounded" (Mark 6:45-52). Jesus the compassionate healer is also the mighty Lord of nature.

The first part of John's gospel is organized around seven progressively more remarkable signs that reveal divine power at work in the world and suggest important truths about Jesus: changing of water into wine at Cana represents the whole transforming mission of Jesus; curing the royal official's son indicates the power of his word; curing the paralytic reminds of his healing power; multiplying the loaves includes the teaching that he is the bread of life; walking on water manifests his power over nature; curing the man born blind suggests his power to cure spiritual blindness; and, finally, raising Lazarus from the dead, the most amazing sign, reveals Jesus as the resurrection and the life. For John, the earthly Jesus was truly the Son of God, who performed marvelous signs revealing the presence of divine power already at work in the world.

Jesus was powerful not only in deed but also in word. His preaching attracted crowds and changed hearts. His parables challenged listeners to radical reflection and suggested ways human beings should be and live in the kingdom of God. He did not simply offer his opinion on disputed topics but rather spoke with absolute authority. His message carried the power of truth and was reinforced by his actions. He spoke often about the need for forgiveness in human affairs, and he himself forgave his enemies, including those responsible for his death. He repudiated violence and refused to resort to violent tactics when the authorities came to arrest him. His teaching on inclusive love of neighbor was strengthened by his personal outreach to excluded persons: women, lepers, tax collectors, foreigners. Matthew presents Jesus as a more powerful teacher than Moses, exemplified by his major discourses, especially the eloquent and insightful Sermon on the Mount (5:1–7:28). At the end of this great sermon, the crowds were astonished at his teaching, just as countless others have been ever since.

The power of Jesus was greater than the sum of his abilities as exorcist, healer, and teacher. He was in his whole being the parable of his Father. He was a unique, concrete embodiment of a divine love that ultimately cannot be defeated. His life and death formed a coherent story of fidelity to his Father that totally identified his person with his mission. The extended encounters between Jesus and various individuals in John's gospel highlight the unparalleled power of his personal presence. For example, his single encounter with the Samaritan woman at the well transformed her whole life, empowering her to spread the Good News in her town where many came to believe in Jesus.

The full power of Jesus is revealed only in his cross and resurrection. Because of his obedient death, God raised him to life so that at his name every knee should bend and every tongue confess that he is Lord (Phil 2:6-11). He is indeed King of Kings and Lord of Lords. History has proven him to be a more influential figure than Herod or even the great Caesar Augustus. Today, around 2.2 billion inhabitants of the earth claim to be his disciples. Jesus, who was empowered by the Spirit as he journeyed to the cross, is now a source of life-giving Spirit for all. Christ's power is no longer limited by time and space. He is now present to human beings in every culture and all historical periods. His message has an enduring power to touch hearts and illumine minds. His grace still empowers those committed to liberating the oppressed, raising up the lowly, and fighting injustice.

A celebration of Christmas that has enduring meaning must move beyond fleeting sentiments to an enduring commitment to the all-powerful Lord and his mission. This personal commitment to Christ challenges us to follow his example by exercising power in constructive ways: resisting the temptation to coerce, control, manipulate, and impress others; relying on the power of self-sacrificing love to help spread the reign of God; doing our part to overcome unjust structures that restrict and exclude others; using economic power to provide a way out for the poor; employing political power to serve the common good and promote justice; and depending on the power of prayer in all that we do. A Christlike use of power is a great way to celebrate the deeper meaning of the birth of Jesus and to maintain the spirit of Christmas in our everyday lives.

The Resurrection as the Spiritual Big Bang

The resurrection of Jesus unleashed an immense spiritual power into the world. Through his death and resurrection, Christ became, as Paul put it, life-giving Spirit. By raising Jesus from the dead, God made his healing and liberating vitality available to all people in all times. The resurrection is a spiritual big bang emitting an unlimited creative energy that fuels the great project of renewing the face of the earth. There is an essential connection between resurrection and mission. The risen Christ empowers his disciples in all ages to carry on his work of spreading the reign of justice and peace in the world. An authentic appropriation of the Easter message sets up a moral obligation to bring Christ's love and forgiveness to all our human relationships. The Easter season challenges us to rise above selfishness and to put the Gospel into practice. To share in the paschal mystery of Christ is to die to the old sinful self and to rise to the new life of generous service to others. The resurrection not only reveals the trustworthy God who vindicated the life and teachings of Jesus, it also empowers disciples to carry on Christ's mission to further the cause of God and humanity.

The story of Simon Peter, the Galilean fisherman who left his livelihood to follow Jesus, exemplifies these claims about the transformative power of the resurrection. The evangelists, especially Matthew, do not hesitate to portray Peter's limitations, weaknesses, and sins. We recall the scene on the Sea of Galilee: the disciples are a few miles offshore and Jesus comes walking toward them on the water. Jesus then invites Peter to walk on the water toward him. Peter starts out well but then becomes frightened and begins to sink. Jesus reaches out to save him but also chides him for his lack of faith and asks why he doubted (Matt 14:22-33). When Jesus first predicts his passion and death, Peter rebukes him, saying God forbid any such thing happen to him. Jesus responds with surprising harshness, calling Peter a Satan and insisting that he is an obstacle to him and his mission. Peter is not in tune with God's will but is expressing his own selfish interests (Matt 16:22-23). In his account of the Last Supper, the evangelist John indicates that Peter still does not understand the servant role of Jesus. The Master begins to wash the feet of the disciples, but Peter insists that he will never wash his feet. After Jesus explains that sharing in his inheritance is at stake, Peter, in his usual impetuous style, says he wants his head and hands washed as well (John 13:1-20). The Last Supper also provides the setting for an emotional exchange between Master and disciple. Jesus tells Peter that this very night, before the cock crows, he will deny him three times. Peter vehemently responds that he is ready to die rather than deny his Lord (Matt 26:31-37). Later in Matthew's passion account, while Jesus is being interrogated by the Sanhedrin, a serving girl accuses Peter of being with Jesus. The man who said he was ready to die for the Master completely crumbles and denies he even knows him—a betrayal repeated twice more, just as the Lord foretold (Matt 26:69-75).

The Gospel of John suggests that even after the resurrection, Peter is slow to understand what has happened. Mary of Magdala goes to the tomb, finds it empty, and reports this to the disciples. Peter and the disciple Jesus loved run to the tomb. The Beloved Disciple arrives first but waits for Peter, who enters and observes the burial clothes. Then the Beloved Disciple goes in, observes the scene, and he believes. We are left with the impression that Peter has not yet grasped the significance of the empty tomb (John 20:1-10).

A decisive turning point for Peter is related in the epilogue of John's gospel (21:1-19). It seems that Peter and some other disciples returned to Galilee and their former occupation as fishermen. One evening Peter decides to go fishing, and six others join him. They catch nothing all night. At dawn the Lord, standing on the shore but unrecognized, tells them to cast their net on the starboard side, and they catch a huge number of fish, 153 large ones. After returning to shore, Peter and his companions share a breakfast of bread and fish prepared by the Master. Peter knows that the Beloved Disciple has correctly identified their host as Jesus himself, but he does not dare to initiate a conversation with him. Finally, the Lord speaks, asking Peter if he loves him more than the other disciples. When Peter responds affirmatively, Christ tells him to "feed my lambs." Twice more the Lord poses the same question to Peter, causing him great distress. We imagine him recalling the three times he denied the Lord, making his thrice-repeated expression of love all the more poignant. Each time, the Lord reminds him that their intimate loving relationship must lead to a life of pastoral service, feeding and tending the lambs and sheep.

This encounter with the risen Christ can be viewed as a remarkable conversion experience for Peter. The doubter who faltered when walking on the water now walks with faith and courage. The disciple who wanted to preserve his master from suffering and death now shares in the power of that obedient act of self-sacrificing love. The man who did not want Jesus to wash his feet now understands the lesson and goes about serving others. The one who succumbed to the slightest pressure from a serving maid now boldly proclaims his faith in Christ before the highest officials. Peter functions as an inspiring example of the immense power of the resurrection to change hearts and strengthen human beings for the great task of spreading the reign of God.

The Acts of the Apostles, the second part of Luke's two-volume work, gives us concrete examples of Peter's life of courageous and faithful service. Soon after the ascension, Peter took charge and led a process of prayerful discernment that chose Mathias to replace Judas as a member of the Twelve (Acts 1:15-20). On Pentecost, the day the Holy Spirit came upon the disciples, Peter preached a powerful sermon that placed Jesus in the context of salvation history and ended with the confident affirmation that God had raised the crucified Jesus to life, constituting him as both Lord and Messiah. On that occasion, about three thousand persons, moved by Peter's words, were baptized and became followers of Christ.

The healing Spirit of the risen Christ found an apt vehicle in Peter. One day Peter and John went to the temple for the three o'clock hour of prayer. A lame beggar over forty years old met them at "the Beautiful Gate" and asked for alms. Peter told him he did not have gold or silver to give him but he would share with him what he had, the healing power of Jesus Christ. After Peter took his right hand and raised him up, his feet and ankles grew strong, and with the two disciples, he entered the temple jumping around and praising God. Peter used the occasion to preach the Good News to the astonished crowd. The God of Abraham had indeed raised Jesus to life, and the risen Lord was the source of the healing power that cured the man crippled from birth (Acts 3:1-26).

While Peter was still speaking, the captain of the temple guard arrested Peter and John and the next day brought them before the Sanhedrin. The high priest and the other leaders were amazed that these uneducated, ordinary companions of Jesus were speaking so boldly and that such a remarkable sign was done through them. Fearful of the impact on the people, they ordered them no longer to speak in the name of Jesus and *threatened them if they did so. No longer intimidated, Peter declared that it was impossible for them not to speak about what they had seen and heard and that they were going to obey God and not the Jewish leaders (Acts 4:1-22).*

Peter's reputation as an instrument of Christ's healing power spread widely. People from towns around Jerusalem brought their sick and placed them on beds and sleeping mats in the street where Peter walked, hoping that his shadow would fall on them and they would be cured (Acts 5:12-16). These wonderful stories, along with others related in Acts, remind us that it was the risen Lord who empowered Peter to carry on his mission of preaching and healing. The resurrection transformed a weak and sinful man into a courageous witness to the truth of the Gospel. The good news of Easter is that Christ can do the same for us, and perhaps already has in ways apparent only to the eyes of faith illumined by prayerful reflection.

The Resurrection and Christian Witness

The Easter season invites reflection on the Christian vocation to give witness to the significance and power of the resurrection. The notion of "giving witness" may be more familiar to Evangelical Protestants than to most Catholics today, but it clearly plays an important role in the New Testament and the Christian tradition. The Greek word "martyr" that is translated "witness," occurs thirty-five times in the New Testament. Its ordinary meaning is to give testimony to what one has seen or heard as happens in a court trial when individuals put their integrity on the line by testifying under oath. Beyond the explicit use of the language of witness, the New Testament often implies that the remarkable victory of Christ over death is good news to be shared. Those who encountered the risen Lord typically felt a responsibility to tell others about this transforming experience. Disciples who came to realize the deeper significance of the resurrection eagerly took up the task of proclaiming the Good News and spreading the reign of justice and peace in the world. In the New Testament, resurrection and witness are essentially linked.

The gospel passage proclaimed at the Easter Vigil (Mark 16:1-7) provides a distinctive perspective on the challenge of witnessing to the risen

Lord. The story is familiar: On Sunday morning, Mary of Magdala and some of her women friends come to the tomb to anoint the body of Jesus. In the tomb they encounter a young man in a white robe who informs them that Jesus has been raised and directs them to go and tell Peter and the other disciples that they will see him in Galilee. Thus Mary and her companions are charged with giving witness to the resurrection, to offer testimony that the tomb was empty. The next verse that completes the story and ends the original text of Mark's gospel is, understandably, omitted from the lectionary reading at the Easter Vigil. With a puzzling abruptness, the evangelist concludes his narrative: "Then they went out and fled from the tomb, seized with trembling and bewilderment. They said nothing to anyone, for they were afraid" (16:8). Scripture scholars suggest that an early Christian author was so perplexed by this strange ending to Mark's gospel that he made a number of additions to the text (16:9-20), drawing on material from the other gospels. The additions, verses that are accepted as part of the canonical Gospel, include another story of an appearance to Mary Magdalene alone who does go and tell the disciples, although they do not believe (16:9-10). At the very least, the original abrupt ending reminds us that giving witness to the resurrection is not always easy. The claim that Jesus has been raised can be bewildering, and the call to give testimony to its meaning can be frightening, just as it was for Mary and her companions. It is also possible that Mark intended his strange ending to function as a prod for other disciples to do what Mary failed to do—namely, to offer testimony to the reality of the resurrection. We could include ourselves in that group of other disciples who are called to overcome confusion and fear and serve as witnesses to the risen Christ.

In the book of Revelation, Jesus himself is called "the faithful witness, the first born of the dead and the ruler of the kings of the earth" (1:5). He has "freed us from our sins by his blood"(1:5) and made us into "priests for his God and Father" (1:6). Jesus gave testimony to the majesty of God by revealing the secrets of the Father and by remaining faithful to the God-given mission that cost him his life. He is the great martyr (witness), the exemplar for all those called to give the ultimate witness by sacrificing their life for the cause of God and the kingdom. As Jesus testified to a God of love who wills the salvation of all, so his followers are to give testimony to Christ who is the parable of the Father, the Word made flesh, the definitive manifestation of divine love.

The Acts of the Apostles, Luke's sequel to his gospel, portrays the apostles as the official witnesses appointed by God of the resurrection of Christ. They testify to what they themselves have seen and heard during the public ministry of Jesus, from his baptism in the Jordan until his ascension into heaven. The risen Christ appeared to them in Jerusalem and promised them the gift of the Holy Spirit, empowering them to be his "witnesses in Jerusalem, throughout Judea and Samaria, and to the ends of the earth" (1:8). On Pentecost they received the promised Spirit symbolized by a strong driving wind and tongues of fire that came to rest on each one of them (2:1-4). Immediately, Peter, along with the Eleven, began to give testimony to the divine plan of salvation that centered on the death and resurrection of Jesus (2:14-41). This original public witness was so exuberant that the listeners thought the disciples were drunk. Peter pointed out that they had not been drinking since it was only nine o'clock in the morning. Rather, their joyful enthusiasm signified that the prophecy of Joel was being fulfilled: "It will come to pass in the last days, God says, that I will pour out a portion of my spirit upon all flesh. Your sons and your daughters shall prophecy, your young men shall see visions, your old men shall dream dreams" (2:17). Filled with the promised Spirit, Peter went on to give eyewitness testimony to Jesus, "a man commended to you by God with mighty deeds, wonders and signs." Speaking boldly, Peter got to the central truth of his testimony. "This man, delivered up by the set plan and foreknowledge of God, you killed, using lawless men to crucify him. But God raised him up, releasing him from the throes of death, because it was impossible for him to be held by it" (2:22-24). Contrasting Jesus with King David who died and remained buried, Peter declared with absolute conviction: "God raised this Jesus; of this we are all witnesses" (2:32). Summarizing his testimony, Peter proclaimed: "Therefore, let the whole house of Israel know for certain that God has made him both Lord and Messiah this Jesus whom you crucified" (2:36).

The response to this original apostolic witness was remarkable. Those assembled were "cut to the heart" and asked what they should do. Peter exhorted them to repent and be baptized, while he "testified with many other arguments" (2:40). About three thousand persons, deeply moved by Peter's testimony, repented their sins and were baptized that day (2:37-41).

This striking story of apostolic witness is a rich resource for reflecting on our own Christian calling to testify to our belief in the risen Christ.

It reminds us that the whole notion of giving witness is well grounded in Scripture and the practice of the first disciples. The apostles established a pattern that has characterized Christian witness ever since. With enthusiastic joy and remarkable courage, they gave testimony in word and deed to the reality of the resurrection and to the impact of the risen Lord on their own lives.

During the first three centuries, the disciples of Jesus faced frequent persecutions, and many died for the faith. They became known as martyrs, because they epitomized Christian witness (martyria)*. Their courageous testimony was a major factor in the spread of Christianity. The Christian apologist Tertullian (c. 160–c. 225) famously expressed this truth: "We multiply wherever we are mown down by you: the blood of Christians is seed."*

After Constantine recognized Christianity as a legitimate religion in the Roman Empire in the fourth century, the persecutions ceased, and Christians no longer could demonstrate their dedication to Christ by dying for their faith. Committed disciples were moved to find other ways of witnessing. Some chose an ascetic lifestyle, living austere lives alone in the desert or in monastic communities. Thus the monk replaced the martyr as the epitome of Christian witness. By taking vows of poverty, chastity, and obedience, monks gave testimony to the transcendent values of the kingdom of God.

Since the Second Vatican Council, Catholics have put more emphasis on witnessing to Christ in daily life in the world and in the ordinary activities of human living. All Christians are called to holiness and to testify to their faith in the risen Lord. The great martyrs past and contemporary remind us that discipleship can be costly and that witnessing involves self-sacrifice. The monks instruct us in the value of regular prayer and a disciplined lifestyle. Still, those of us living in the world today must find our own way of testifying to our faith in Christ. In giving witness, we do well to concentrate on the essentials of our faith. With the apostles, we testify to the meaning and power of the death and resurrection of Jesus in our own lives. Testimony rings true when it comes from the heart and reflects our deep-set convictions. Authentic witness is rooted in personal experience. In most cases, Christians testify to Christ more by good example then by lofty rhetoric. Actions do speak louder than words, especially in a culture threatened by skepticism and cynicism.

Examples of effective Christian witness to the resurrection abound in our day. Individuals who retain a joyful spirit while carrying heavy crosses give witness to the triumph of Christ over all the dark forces. Parents who pass on the core of Christian faith to their offspring testify to the centrality of the resurrection. Christians who work consistently for justice and peace give testimony to the risen Christ as the compassionate liberator. Believers who are good stewards of the earth reflect the resurrection truth that all creation will share in the final victory of the sons and daughters of God. Industrious persons who meet their daily responsibilities and do their work well testify that the resurrection gives a deeper meaning to all of our ordinary activities. Those who face death gracefully enable others to believe that the risen Christ has indeed conquered death itself. Courageous people who explicitly profess their faith in Christ before skeptics and scoffers give witness to the strengthening power of the resurrection. Christians who continue to pray when God is silent exemplify the Easter conviction that the Father of Jesus is entirely trustworthy. Examples like these prompt further reflection on ways all of us can give more effective witness to the impact of the risen Christ on our lives.

Ecumenical and Interfaith Dialogue

Ever since I was ordained in 1962, ecumenism has been high on my priority list. In my three parish assignments, I felt blessed and enriched by my regular meetings with Protestant ministers and other Catholic priests in the area. We prayed together, offered mutual support, sponsored common worship services, and collaborated on projects to serve the common good. For me these interactions were personally life-giving and energizing.

Rahner left me with a broad ecumenical perspective and motivation for maintaining the effort on behalf of Christian unity. His anthropology stresses our shared nature as self-transcendental beings; his theology of God prompts discussion of diverse images of God; his theology of grace alerts us to the presence of the Spirit in other Christian churches; his theology of salvation avoids religious exclusivism; his Christology reminds of our most fundamental shared beliefs; his ecclesiology focuses on what various churches hold in common; his sacramentology suggests common ground on disputed issues; and his eschatology reminds us that Christian unity is God's gift to us that will be complete only at the end time. These themes form the background for this article.

Renewing Ecumenical Passion

In his farewell at the Last Supper, Jesus prayed that his followers would all be one, united with him and with one another (John 17:20-23). His vision was one shepherd and one flock united by the sound of his voice (John 10:16). Today, when peace in the world is threatened by religious tensions, it is more important than ever to heed the voice of Christ calling for Christian unity. Unfortunately, it seems the ecumenical movement has lost momentum at a time when our fragmented world most needs a united Christian witness.

Some critics claim that Christ's prayer for unity is being ignored by church leaders, especially the Vatican, while others contend that the very ideal of one flock has been lost among evangelical Christians. Over the last couple decades, we have indeed lost some of the passion that energized the ecumenical movement in the heady period after the Second Vatican Council. In those days, many people experienced the thrill of discovering common teachings and practices shared with their Christian brothers and sisters in other denominations. Living-room dialogues drew people from different Christian backgrounds into stimulating religious conversations. Pulpit exchanges provided fresh perspectives on common Scripture readings. Collaborative efforts on behalf of justice and peace proved to be more effective. Those of us who participated in ecumenical activities during those days can remember the exhilaration of establishing friendships and working relationships with long-estranged brothers and sisters in Christ. I myself have fond memories of a courageous Lutheran pastor who, despite long-standing prejudices and social taboos still operative in Sandusky, Ohio, in the 1960s, befriended me as a young priest newly arrived in town and invited me to join a discussion group of local ministers who met at his church. Those discussions were eye opening for me and left me with an enduring appreciation of the importance and value of ecumenical dialogue.

That honeymoon period, however, is over, never to be repeated. Younger people have reaped the benefits of that intense period of ecumenical progress without having known the excitement of blazing new trails. The amazing progress toward Christian unity made in the decades after the council set up expectations for full visible unity that have not been fulfilled. Christian churches remain divided, and the Lord's Supper continues to be a sign of separation rather than a cause of unity. This situation is disappointing to veterans of the movement and simply unintelligible to others, especially those who grew up in an open ecumenical atmosphere that emphasized common bonds and fostered tolerance of differences.

The honeymoon may be over, but the ecumenical movement is not totally dead. The enthusiasm may have diminished, but the Spirit is still moving the church toward the ideal of one flock and one shepherd. Grassroots ecumenism is now an accepted part of the religious landscape. In communities all over the country, Christians gather for common prayer services on special occasions such as Good Friday and Memorial Day. They work together to feed the hungry and shelter the homeless. Pastors of various denominations meet regularly to discuss the common Lectionary readings for the following Sunday. Local examples of ecumenical progress come to mind. A group of Presbyterians chose to hold an important regional meeting in a Catholic church as a sign of common bonds and a renewed commitment to Christian unity. A group of evangelical leaders invited a Catholic theologian to give a talk explaining the practice of signing with ashes on Ash Wednesday and then held an ecumenical service built around this traditional practice. The fact that this kind of ecumenical activity is now taken for granted should not obscure its crucial importance in furthering the cause of Christian unity.

Although the ecumenical movement has not achieved institutional unity, church leaders have made some important initial moves. In his remarkable 1995 encyclical Ut Unum Sint *(That All May Be One), Pope John Paul II invited leaders and theologians in other churches to engage with him in a fraternal dialogue on how the Petrine ministry (the office of the pope) could be exercised in a way that is more acceptable and more conducive to the cause of unity. Three decades earlier, Pope Paul VI and Patriarch Athenagoras I of Constantinople rescinded the mutual excommunications the Catholic Church and the Orthodox Church had imposed on each other at the beginning of the second millennium in 1054. This historic reconciling gesture between the sister churches of the East and*

West opened up the possibility of restoring the kind of visible unity in legitimate diversity that prevailed during the first millennium of Christian history. Unfortunately, this marvelous opportunity for the universal church to breathe out of both lungs (an image favored by John Paul II) has run into many religious and political obstacles—for example, the more visible role of Eastern churches in union with Rome after the breakup of the Soviet Union. Little progress toward institutional unity has been made, adding to the general feeling that the ecumenical movement has stalled.

Ecumenism includes not only grassroots cooperation and official interactions among leaders but also theological discussions. Since 1968, Catholic theologians have participated regularly in multilateral dialogues sponsored by the Faith and Order Commission of the World Council of Churches. In 1982, over one hundred theologians representing most major church traditions, including Catholic, met in Lima, Peru, and produced a document titled Baptism, Eucharist, and Ministry (BEM) that offers a consensus summary of what Christians hold in common on baptism, Eucharist, and ministry. Five years later, after extensive consultation, the Vatican issued a detailed response praising the document for its contributions to Christian unity but noting that some of its points do not accord with full Catholic teaching and need further study. The Vatican response produced widespread disappointment among theologians, and little progress on that dialogue has been made since.

Catholic theologians are also involved in many bilateral discussions with other Christian communities, including Anglican, Lutheran and Methodist. After years of intensive work, the Catholic-Lutheran dialogue produced a remarkable consensus statement on justification, the key issue that divided the two churches since the Reformation in the sixteenth century. In essence, the document affirms that we are justified by faith through God's grace and this should lead to good works as the fruit of justification. Within this shared understanding, Catholics and Lutherans still have differences in language, explanation, and emphasis, but the issue of justification need no longer divide the two churches. On Reformation Sunday, 1999, in Augsburg, Germany, representatives of the Lutheran World Federation and the Vatican officially signed the Joint Declaration on the Doctrine of Justification, unleashing new ecumenical energy around the world. For example, two years later in my home diocese of Toledo, Bishop James Hoffman and Bishop Marcus Lohrmann of the

Northwest Ohio Synod of the Evangelical Lutheran Church in America entered an official covenant, pledging mutual efforts to heed Christ's call for unity by praying and studying together and working collaboratively to help those in need. In this case, a theological breakthrough that received official recognition paved the way for practical cooperation at the local level. The hard work of theological dialogue is continuing behind the scenes. Members of the Catholic-Methodist dialogue in the United States, for example, meet twice a year, present position papers on a specific topic, such as the role of the church in the world, and over a period of about five years try to produce a statement summarizing areas of convergence and points of disagreement. The hope is that this kind of careful, patient theological work will prepare for eventual unity and, in the meantime, open up opportunities for collaborative efforts.

Two decades ago, the influential theologian Karl Rahner advanced the thesis that institutional unity between the Catholic Church and the mainline Protestant churches was actually possible and could be achieved in a relatively short period of time. Rahner had in mind a conciliar fellowship in which all the partner churches accept the unifying role of the Petrine office as well as the fundamental truths expressed in Scripture and the traditional creeds, while maintaining their distinctive structures and practices. This relatively brief period has elapsed without significant progress toward institutional unity, and with no imminent breakthroughs on the horizon. It is not surprising that some feel an ecumenical winter has descended upon us. Given all the disappointments, it is important to recall the signs of ecumenical hope, especially in the lived experience of ordinary Christians who pray and work together and in the theological dialogues that are gradually reconciling the issues that divide the churches. Ultimately, our hope is in Christ, the Good Shepherd whose voice has an inherent power to draw estranged Christians into unity.

At the University of Toledo, I was also very involved in interfaith dialogue. In the late 1990s, students on campus sponsored a series of Catholic-Muslim dialogues that enabled me to enter into discussions with Muslim scholars. These initial discussions, often polemical in tone, produced a good deal of passionate response. As time went on, the dialogues became less polemical and more inclusive of Jews,

Christians, and Muslims. Participants were more open to learning from one another and looking for common ground. Eventually, the University of Toledo established a Center for Religious Understanding that sponsored a whole series of interfaith events and enabled students from diverse traditions to get to know one another and to collaborate on joint projects. Over the years, my relationship with the Jewish and Muslim communities grew, and solid friendships formed. In my interfaith presentations, I often paraphrase Hans Kung: No peace among the nations without peace among the religions; no peace among the religions without genuine dialogue; no genuine dialogue without honest self-criticism. We can all rejoice when genuine dialogue leads to collaborative efforts on behalf of justice and peace. When the Abrahamic family experiences healing, the whole world benefits. In all my interfaith activities, Rahner's theology alerts me to signs of hope that we can achieve greater unity as the following article suggests.

Christian-Muslim Dialogue: Islamic Perspectives

At the end of the 2007 Ramadan fast, 138 Muslim leaders sent a letter titled A Common Word between Us and You *to Pope Benedict, the Orthodox patriarch of Constantinople, and the archbishop of Canterbury, as well as many other leaders of Christian denominations. The opening paragraph points out that Muslims and Christians together constitute well over half of the world's population and insists that "there can be no meaningful peace in the world" without "peace and justice between these two religious communities."*[18] *The letter goes on to argue at length that the solid basis for ongoing dialogue and collaboration is our common commitment to loving the one God wholeheartedly and to loving our neighbor as ourselves.*

Commentators and respondents have noted the historic significance of this Muslim initiative, the first collective outreach in the 1,400-year history shared by Christianity and Islam. It is a remarkable achievement in itself for the Islamic community, which has no unifying leader like a pope or patriarch, to come to such a broad consensus among both Sunni and Shia scholars and officials from countries all over the globe. The inviting tone has elicited positive responses from many Christian leaders, including Cardinal Jean-Louis Tauran, president of the Pontifical Council for Inter-religious Dialogue, who described the initiative as "a positive signal." Rowan Williams, archbishop of Canterbury, said the call for "respect, peace and goodwill should now be taken up by Christians and Muslims at all levels and in all countries." David Coffey, head of the Baptist World Alliance, personally welcomed the letter as "a groundbreaking initiative" that could be "a major contribution" to "religious liberty and world peace."

The enthusiastic responses are based not only on the tone of A Common Word but also its content. The authors have identified genuine common ground between Christians and Muslims that is solidly rooted in our sacred texts. Love of God and love of neighbor are essential core elements in both traditions and form a firm foundation for dialogue and collaboration on behalf of justice and peace in the world. Constructive Christian-Muslim dialogues can focus on various similarities: for instance, mutual respect for Jesus and Muhammad; the wisdom found in the Bible and the Quran; the relationship between Lent and Ramadan; the importance of daily prayer; and the role of pilgrimages. However, the letter wisely focuses on a teaching especially familiar to Christians, the commandment of Jesus to love God wholeheartedly and our neighbor as ourselves. The burden of the letter, then, is to demonstrate to Christian readers that this dual command is also central to Islam.

The long section of the letter on love of God explicates a saying of Muhammad: "The best that I have said—myself and the prophets that came before me—is: 'There is no god but God, he alone, he hath no associate, his is the sovereignty and his is the praise and he hath power over all things.'" This calls Muslims to devote their minds and hearts to God alone, with gratitude and trust and without any rival in their souls. The first chapter of the Holy Quran begins with a passage frequently recited by Muslims: "In the name of God, the infinitely good, the all-merciful. Praise be to God, the Lord of the worlds. The infinitely good, the all-merciful. Owner of the Day of Judgment. Thee we worship, and thee we ask for help. Guide us upon the straight path" (1:1-6). Later, the Quran enjoins: "So invoke the name of the Lord and devote thyself to him with a complete devotion" (73:8). The letter notes that for Muslims this means "all the faculties and powers of their soul must be totally devoted and attached to God." Muhammad, who serves as a role model for Muslims, states, "My living and my dying are for God" (6:162), and declares to all: "If ye love God, follow me; God will love you and forgive you your sins. God is forgiving, merciful" (3:31). In Islam, love of God is "not a mere fleeting, partial emotion"; it is "an injunction requiring all-embracing, constant and active love of God" inspired by frequent repetition of the formula, "there is no god but God."

After recalling this core Islamic teaching on love of God, the authors of the letter express their belief that it can be equated with the first and greatest commandment taught by Jesus to love God with all our heart, soul, mind, and strength (Mark 12:28-29). Remarkably, they even suggest that Muhammad was "perhaps, through inspiration, restating and alluding to the Bible's First Commandment."

The section on love of neighbor is much shorter but makes the clear claim that, for Muslims, "love of neighbor is an essential and integral part of faith in God," because "in Islam without love of the neighbor there is no true faith in God and no righteousness." Muhammad insisted: "None of you has faith until you love for your brother what you love for yourself." This love cannot be limited to mere sympathy but must include "generosity and self-sacrifice." Thus, the Quran commands giving of one's wealth "to kinsfolk, orphans, the needy, wayfarers and those who ask" (2:177). Once again, the letter points to a similar teaching in the Bible, recalling the teaching of Jesus that the second greatest commandment is like the first: You shall love your neighbor as yourself (Matt 22:38-40)—a command found also in the Hebrew Scriptures (Lev 19:17-18).

In the third and final section, A Common Word admits that we cannot minimize the real differences between Islam and Christianity but at the same time affirms the common ground we share in the two great commandments. The discovery of common teaching is not surprising since the Quran itself says that Muhammad taught "nothing fundamentally or essentially new," but only what was said to messengers before him (41:43). The Quran declares to Jews and Christians: "Come to a common word between us and you" (3:64)—a marvelous phrase that serves as an appropriate title of the open letter. Based on the Quranic teaching "let there be no compulsion in religion" (2:256), the letter suggests that adherents of the three monotheistic religions "should be free to each follow what God commanded them." The Muslim authors of the letter want all Christians to know "that we are not against them and that Islam is not against them"—as long as they do not wage war or oppress Muslims. They also *suggest that Christians need not be against Muslims, citing the saying of Jesus: "For he who is not against us is on our side" (Mark 9:40).*

Finally, A Common Word *invites Christians "to come together with us on the common essentials of our two religions" and let love of God and neighbor be "the basis of all future interfaith dialogue." The stakes are high: "If Muslims and Christians are not at peace, the world cannot be at peace." At the end of the letter, we find the message that a world weary of terrorism has been waiting to hear from Muslim leaders: To those who "relish conflict and destruction" in itself or as a tactical weapon, "we say that our very eternal souls are at stake if we fail to sincerely make every effort to make peace and come together in harmony." Our differences must not cause "hatred and strife between us." "Let us vie with each other only in righteousness and good works. Let us respect each other, be fair, just and kind to another and live in sincere peace, harmony and mutual good will."*

This message is indeed timely and bold. Let us pray that it will elicit constructive responses from all Christians and Muslims and lead to collaborative efforts for justice and peace in the world.

Since then, Christian/Muslim relationships have taken a few hard blows: for instance, the questionable language of Pope Benedict at Regensburg and the persecution of Coptic Christian churches in Egypt. Nevertheless, the "Common Word" letter remains an important basis for dialogue in the future.

Defending Belief

Much of my ministry has taken place in a university setting. I served as a campus minister for twelve years at Bowling Green State University and for thirty years at the University of Toledo. In those settings, questions about fundamental Christian beliefs, including the existence of God, often came to my attention. When I was teaching the course Belief and Unbelief, students talked to me outside of class about their own problems with belief in God. Collegians faced with new challenges to their faith sought my advice on how to make sense of the belief system received from their parents. Atheistic professors looked for opportunities to discuss core beliefs with me as a priest and theologian. Catholic faculty members, highly educated in their field but lacking a mature understanding of their faith, asked for suggestions on deepening their knowledge of their religious heritage. Periodically, I wrote articles that I could share with individuals seeking guidance on faith questions.

Responding to the New Atheism

In the past decade, a number of books have been published that vigorously attack belief in God as delusional and dangerous. Among the more popular: The End of Faith: Religious Terror and the Future of Religion, *by Sam Harris (2004);* Breaking the Spell: Religion as a Natural Phenomenon, *by Daniel Dennett (2006);* The God Delusion, *by Richard Dawkins (2006); and* God Is not Great: How Religion Poisons Everything, *by Christopher Hitchens (2007). This "new atheism," as the phenomenon is commonly called, attacks popular forms of religion that are considered dehumanizing, as well as Christian and Muslim fundamentalism that promotes fanaticism and violence. In general, these authors do not engage the more sophisticated theological defenses of theism proposed by contemporary theologians, such as Karl Rahner and Paul Tillich, but are content to target popular forms of belief.*

We call these authors "new atheists" in relation to the classic critics of the nineteenth and twentieth centuries who attacked religion and belief. The father of all modern atheism is Ludwig Feuerbach (1804–1872), who was baptized Catholic and raised Protestant. As a student at the University of Berlin in 1824, he attended lectures by the philosopher Hegel (1770–1830), who was proposing a comprehensive philosophy of religion that understood God not as a supreme being above or outside this world but as the Absolute Spirit immanently present in world history and human existence. In his influential work The Essence of Christianity, *Feuerbach went a step further and insisted that all talk about God was really talk about ourselves, a projection of our own desires. His aim was "to change the friends of God into friends of man, believers into thinkers, worshipers into workers, candidates for the other world into students of this world, Christians who on their confession are half-animals and half-angels into men—whole men." Karl Marx, born a Jew and raised*

Christian, was also a member of the "left wing Hegelians" at the University of Berlin. Under Feuerbach's influence, he adopted an atheistic philosophy that he eventually applied to the plight of the working poor in his 1848 Manifesto of the Communist Party. *According to Marx, religion is "the opiate of the people," a drug that diverts the attention of believers from the real problems of this world to the future joys of heaven. Thus, "the abolition of religion as the illusory happiness of the people is required for their real happiness." His great hope for progress toward a more humane world was the proletarian revolution that would fundamentally alter economic arrangements and produce a classless society. In this situation there would be no need to fight theism; religion would simply wither away.*

Ludwig Feuerbach's contention that theism is a projection of our desires was taken up and developed by Sigmund Freud (1856–1939), the founder of modern psychoanalysis. Freud, who was raised as a Jew and was periodically taken to Catholic Mass by his Czech nanny, eventually adopted a scientific worldview that left no room for theism. In his 1927 book The Future of an Illusion, *he offered a sharp critique of religious belief. Religious ideas, including belief in God, have no rational basis; rather, "they are illusion, fulfillment of the oldest, strongest, and most urgent wishes of mankind." Human beings desire a father figure to protect them in their helplessness and so project the existence of a powerful God to watch over them. Such illusions based on projection are essentially dehumanizing; they keep believers in an "infantile state." For Freud, religion is "a universal obsessional neurosis" that has failed to bring true happiness to the human race.*

The new atheists, who share the conviction that belief is dehumanizing, are very aggressive in opposing theism and proposing a contemporary version of atheism. To take a prime example, Richard Dawkins, in his The God Delusion, *seeks to prove that belief in God is "highly improbable" and that atheism is the best option for making the world more humane. Dawkins, a renowned Oxford professor and evolutionary biologist, argues that atheists are morally superior to theists and that the more educated and intelligent people are, the more likely they are to reject belief in God. He claims, for example, that less than 10 percent of Nobel scientists are theists. Along this line, he argues that Albert Einstein was not a believer in God despite his many positive comments about religion, including his famous statement: "Science without religion is lame, religion without science is blind."*

The attacks Dawkins makes on religious beliefs are harsh indeed. His description of the God of the Old Testament is especially caustic: "the most unpleasant character in all fiction: jealous and proud of it; a petty, unjust, unforgiving control freak; a vindictive, bloodthirsty ethnic cleanser; a misogynistic, homophobic, racist, infanticidal, genocidal, filicidal, pestilential, megalomaniacal, sadomasochistic, capriciously malevolent bully." He is no less harsh in his appraisal of the God of the New Testament who appears in the gospels as "vicious, sadomasochistic and repellent." This God incarnates himself so that he can be tortured and executed to make up for the sin of Adam that afflicts all human beings. For Dawkins, the Father of Jesus is not only a masochist but also a vengeful God who is seriously offended by sin and demands harsh acts of atonement.

Dawkins attacks some of the popular forms of theism that have developed over the centuries, including the God of modern Deists who is the "omega of mathematicians, a hyper-engineer who detonated the big bang and then retired and was never heard from again." God is an underachiever who fails to answer prayers. In support of this point, Dawkins refers to a scientific study demonstrating that the Royal Family in England is no healthier than other sample families, despite prayers for them in churches all over England every Sunday. The God Delusion frequently makes fun of popular belief. After surviving an assassination attempt, Pope John Paul II stated his belief that Our Lady of Fatima saved his life: "A maternal hand guided the bullet." Dawkins sarcastically asks why Mary, while she was at it, didn't guide it to miss him completely. Even Mother Teresa of Calcutta is not beyond his scorn for believers. Reacting to her conviction that widespread abortion is a threat to world peace, Dawkins characterized her as "sanctimoniously hypocritical" and her judgments as "cockeyed."

The attempt of Richard Dawkins to disprove the traditional theistic arguments and to demonstrate that belief in God is delusional, i.e., a persistent false belief despite contrary evidence, is not very sophisticated. He enters the field of theology as an amateur, not prepared to deal with its tradition of deep and complex discussions on the topic of belief. The literary critic Terry Eagleton describes The God Delusion as "a vulgar caricature of religious faith that would make a first-year theology student wince." On the other hand, it is important to provide a Christian response to the atheistic criticism of popular belief. There is no doubt that projection plays a role in developing an image of God, and clearly some believers *hold superstitious views and exhibit infantile behavior. At the same time, we all know believers who seem relatively healthy and function as mature adults. Furthermore, we honor great saints who have demonstrated outstanding human virtues: for instance, the intellectual integrity of Thomas Aquinas and the spiritual balance of Teresa of Avila.*

The new atheists challenge all of us to refine our understanding of the Deity. In the best of the Christian tradition, God is not perceived as a being among other beings, nor as a more intelligent and more powerful being than the most advanced human being. Rather, God is the ultimate Source of all existence, the final Goal of all human striving, the transcendent Creator of all finite creatures, the incomprehensible Mystery beyond all words, images, and categories, the gracious Ground of all being, and the inexhaustible Fountain of all love.

All descriptions of a harsh and punishing God in the Bible should be interpreted in the light of the God of love proclaimed by Jesus, the trustworthy Father who raised him to life. From the perspective of the resurrection, we must find alternate explanations of the violence attributed to God in the Scriptures. It might be, for example, due to the common practice of applying human characteristics to God or the natural tendency to mobilize divine authority to justify questionable human behavior. The Father of Jesus loves all people without exception and wants human beings to flourish. God knows us by name and invites us to develop our talents and gifts to the fullest degree, to actualize our potential, to become all that we can be. "The glory of God is the human person fully alive," as well expressed by Irenaeus of Lyons (c. 130–c. 200). Far from stunting human development, Christian theism involves a call to maturity and provides motivation to move beyond childish ways toward true adulthood.

Contemporary liberation theology has taken the Marxist critique of religion seriously and has championed the cause of creating a more just social order. This theology, practiced by Gustavo Gutierrez, Elizabeth Johnson, and James Cone, among many others, celebrates the God who freed the Israelites from slavery and gave them social, economic, and political freedom. Yahweh spoke through the prophets, insisting that his people work for justice and attend to the widows, orphans, and aliens. God sent Jesus to preach the Good News to the poor and to free the captives. Christ identified himself with the hungry and thirsty and challenged his followers to care for those in need. Liberation theology has refocused these important biblical themes that have prompted Christians for two millennia to work for justice and peace, including the vast number of anonymous laborers in the social arena as well as the recognized prophets like Francis of Assisi, Catherine of Siena, Martin Luther King, and Dorothy Day. For them, theism was obviously not an opiate but rather a catalyst for fighting social sin and expanding the kingdom of justice and peace. Not all Christians have understood the social thrust of the Gospel or lived it out, but growing numbers of believers, including young people, are involved in justice and peace projects, suggesting the ongoing power of faith to motivate and guide the effort to humanize our world. Considering the obvious failures of Marxism and the limitations of the secular humanism espoused by Dawkins and the new atheism, a plausible argument can be made that Christian theism remains a richer resource for constructing a more humane world.

Societal and Cultural Issues

Some of my monthly "Reflections" articles have responded to current social and cultural topics, including the Iraq War, the civil rights movement, the art of Picasso, and the Olympic Games. In addressing these issues, Rahner's theology has functioned like a powerful searchlight that illumines the deeper ways that grace and sin are contending in contemporary society and culture. Here is an example of how the Rahnerian perspective alerted me to the spiritual aspects of a contemporary writer.

The Spirituality of John Updike

For over half a century, John Updike wrote with brilliance and insight about sex, religion, and art, which he called "the three great secret things in human experience." With his death in January 2009 at the age of 76, we lost a keen observer of the human scene and a gifted writer who alerted us to the ambiguities of the human soul with its "Rembrantesque blacks and whites" and reminded us of the "majestic significance" of our daily "decisions and recognitions." Updike was a prolific author, publishing over sixty books and hundreds of essays, short stories, and reviews. The

*novelist Philip Roth called him "our time's greatest man of letters" and
an enduring "national treasure." Despite the charge of some critics that
Updike was stronger on style than on content, his vast corpus actually
contains some profound insights that illumine the spiritual search for
meaning and purpose in a world that often appears absurd and random.*

*Writing about religion was grounded for Updike in his lifelong rela-
tionship with various Protestant churches, which he described in a 1999
essay, "The Future of Faith" (cf.* Due Considerations, *pp. 27–41). John
was confirmed about the age of fourteen and attended services regularly
with his father, even though his head "brimmed with non-Christian
images" such as "girls, cartoons, and baseball." From his father he got
the sense of the Christian religion not as a repressive institution but "as
something weak and tenuous and in need of rescue." During his college
years at Harvard and later living in New York, he continued attending
Lutheran services, feeling "cleansed and lightened, and taking a certain
contrarian pride in participating in ceremonies that, by the wisdom of
the world, were profitless and irrational." During his adult life, Updike
usually attended Sunday worship alone, a practice that seemed like "an
annoying affectation" to his consorts and left "little trace" in the spiritual
lives of his children. Nevertheless, church attendance provided him with
"an inner sense of contact" that could be expressed as "knowing Christ,"
and the feeling that his life was "being shaped, broadly, by transactions
with the supernatural." For him there was "no other game in the existential arena than the Christian creed, no other answer to the dread one's
mortal existence brings with it."*

*John Updike knew firsthand the dread and terror that stalks the human
family. As a young man he periodically felt a vivid sense that "we are all
poised above the chasm of our eventual deaths." These terrifying experiences were like being "suddenly flayed of the skin of habit and herd feeling
that customarily enwraps and deadens our deep predicament." On one
occasion, when he was in his mid-thirties, the terror attacked him as he
prepared for sleep in a dormitory room of a New England college where
he had done a reading that evening. In the midst of his terror, he spotted
on a bookshelf a self-help book with a "pious flavor"—the kind of book he
would not ordinarily read or respect. He read a few pages that surprisingly allayed his "impatient groveling anxiety," enabling him to sleep.
It was the "uncanny" availability of the unlikely book that made the
experience so remarkable for him. In this vignette, we get a glimpse of*

Updike's personal demons and of his propensity to detect a mysterious benign power at work in the struggles of life.

Much later in his life, in his middle sixties, Updike had another encounter with his demon in a hotel room in Florence. During the night he felt "fearful, and adrift, failed." His anxiety was intensified by the prospect of having to write an article on the future of faith—a task that might, "empty out of me the last drops of what feeble faith had got me this far." He prayed for the gift of sleep to relieve his anxiety, "without expecting the prayer to be answered." At this point, he looked out his hotel window as an intense rainstorm with lightning and gusty winds bombarded the city, including the giant dome of the Duomo, the major church in the city. Despite this bombardment, "the hulking old cathedral, crouched like a stoic, mute dragon" withstood the attack. As this scene unfolded before his eyes, he knew "he was not alone in the universe" and was filled with "a glad sense that God was at work" in "this Jacobean wrestle" between the "heavenly wrath" of the storm and the "architectural defiance" of the Duomo. Then he fell asleep, feeling like the whole event was "a transaction, a rescue," an answered prayer. In this more mature religious experience, Updike explicitly identifies the mysterious power at work in the world as the God of Christian faith.

The personal witness to tested faith offered by John Updike, in "the empirical style of American religion," invites further reflection on the common spiritual adventure. His experience of dread reminds us of the many faces of anxiety that emerge in confrontation with the dark realities of failure, finitude, meaninglessness, and the mystery of death. Escape from anxiety is a common tactic in the modern world. For Updike, the great escape mechanism is illicit sex. It is for good reason that he has been called the "great chronicler of suburban adultery." His books are filled with vivid descriptions of sexual encounters—"a grand surprise nature has cooked up for us" with "its accelerated pulse rate and the drastic overestimation of the love object, the rhythmic build-up and discharge: but then that's it." Updike is masterful in unmasking the rationalizations surrounding sex. In his novel A Month of Sundays, *the married, womanizing pastor, Reverend Tom Marshfield, sent by his bishop to a desert retreat for rehabilitation, writes a weekly sermon as part of his therapy. In a grand refusal to face his sinfulness, he composes an ingenious sermon arguing that Jesus approved of adultery and that adultery that brings together "insatiable egos and workable genitals" should be* considered one of the sacraments of the church. *Reverend Marshfield summarizes his comical, but ultimately sad, rationalization: "Verily the sacrament of marriage, as instituted in its adamant impossibility by our Savior, exists but as a precondition for the sacrament of adultery." In Updike, sex is a metaphor for all the dark forces that tempt us to egocentricity and manipulation of others—tendencies frequently hidden by rationalization. Reading Updike from this perspective can prompt honest self-examination as well as a critical analysis of societal trends, including the casual sex of the "hooking-up" youth culture.*

Christian spirituality as lived experience reflects our perception of God. Updike himself was very influenced by the writings of the Swiss Reformed theologian Karl Barth (1884–1986), a great critic of liberal Protestant theology and the founder of the Neo-Orthodox movement in theology. Updike was fascinated with Barth's notion of God as the "Wholly Other," the hidden God who is accessible only through the Christ witnessed in the Scriptures and not through science or philosophy. The protagonist in Updike's novel Roger's Version *is Roger Lambert, a former Methodist pastor who migrated to academe as a professor of theology. He enunciates a consistent Barthian position in his ongoing argument with a young computer expert Dale Kohler, who claims he can prove God exists from the new physics and sophisticated computer analyses. Lambert, who loved Barth's "magnificent seamless integrity," quotes the Swiss theologian to seal his argument with Kohler: "The god who stood at the end of some human way would not be God." For a Barthian, trying to prove God's existence through science is a fatally flawed project.*

Updike, who had a vast knowledge of the Christian theological tradition, reminds us that the great saints and theologians all recognized the limitations of our words and images in describing God. Aquinas, for example, said that the most important thing that we can know about God is that we don't know God. Updike's statements that we are not alone in the universe and have transactions with the supernatural point to a God who is partially revealed but remains ultimately hidden.

Karl Barth's emphasis on "the otherness of God" frees us, according to Updike, to be "exceptionally appreciative and indulgent of this world." Just as Barth appreciated humor, friendships, art, entertainment, and especially the music of Mozart, so believers in the Wholly Other find "permission to live," to exult in the joys and sorrows of life on this hard earth. Some critics claim Updike's God is too complacent, allowing us to live too easily with injustice. Clearly, Updike was not a great champion of liberation theology, but his Barthian understanding of the hidden God challenges all idols, including various forms of exclusion, prejudice, and injustice.

Updike suggests some fresh ways of reflecting on our relationship with Christ. In one of his therapeutic sermons, Reverend Marshfield meditates on the miracles of Christ. He recognizes Jesus as a true miracle worker: "for our Lord produces miracles as naturally as the Earth produces flowers." During his ministry, "miracles fell from him as drops of water escape between the fingers of a man drinking from his cupped hand." The problem is the selectivity of Jesus: "if these few, why not all ailing from the beginning of human time?" Why "are we not moved to revolt and overthrow this minute and arbitrary aristocracy of the healed," who happened to live during Jesus' public ministry? After giving voice to this protest against the randomness of human suffering, Marshfield responds that the purpose of the miracles was not alleviation of illness but "demonstration." They were signs of the presence of God's reign in the world, demonstrating a "Law and Ground beyond." Through Marshfield, Updike also invites us to contemplate the miracles from the viewpoint of the one who worked them. Consider Jesus, "his powers green and unproven," risking failure in his bold resolve to turn water into wine at Cana. From this perspective, we marvel at "His daring" and "His perfect and playful faith," and we better understand his stern criticism of his disciples who manifested little faith.

Drawing on his own experience and his remarkable powers of observation, John Updike had a profound understanding of the religious dimension of human existence. His fiction, as well as his essays, contain nuggets of wisdom that illumine the common struggle to face our demons honestly and to stay alert for the hidden transactions with the supernatural that pervade ordinary life.

Classic Paradigms

In addition to guidance on specific ministerial tasks, such as preaching, spiritual direction, catechetical instruction, confessional practice, ecumenical relations, and burying the dead, Rahner gave me a consistent, comprehensive framework (a new paradigm as theologians call it) for understanding and practicing priestly ministry in the contemporary world. In the seminary, I was fortunate to study

Thomistic theology directly from the Latin *Summa* and not only through the manualists. In those days, however, I was not able to appreciate the genius and achievement of Aquinas, nor did I find his classical paradigm very helpful when I began my priestly ministry. This set the stage for my efforts to find a more effective pastoral theology.

In the history of Christianity, a relatively small number of theologians have produced new theological paradigms, fresh ways of understanding and explaining the Christian faith as a whole. A typical list includes: Origen (c. 185–c. 254), who made use of neoplatonic philosophy to explain the Christian message; Augustine (354–430), who infused Western theology with Latin categories and Roman habits of mind; Aquinas (1225–1274), who employed the newly recovered philosophy of Aristotle to create a comprehensive Christian synthesis; Martin Luther (1483–1546), who presented the Christian message from the perspective of grace, faith, and Scripture alone; Friedrich Schleiermacher (1768–1834), who reinterpreted Christian doctrine in response to the challenges of the modern world; Karl Barth (1886–1968), who rejected liberal Protestant theology and started the neo-Orthodox movement; and Hans Urs von Balthasar (1905–1988), who began his theological trilogy by examining the Christian tradition from the perspective of beauty. Most theologians today would agree that Karl Rahner belongs in that elite group.

Rahner's Paradigm

From the beginning of my ministry, Rahner's occasional articles, sermons, and prayers helped me to respond to particular pastoral challenges. It was his publication of *Foundations of Christian Faith* in 1978 that helped me appreciate the new theological paradigm he created. In dialogue with the Christian tradition and the modern world, he refocused our understanding of the faith as a whole and reinterpreted Christian doctrines to make them more intelligible and credible for people influenced by our secular age. His refocusing begins with a Christian anthropology that recognizes the human drive for knowledge and love as well as our social nature as interdependent persons. God is the name we give to the Holy Mystery that encompasses us, the Source of our dynamism and the Goal of our deep longings. Borrowing from the Eastern fathers, Rahner treats grace as God's gratuitous self-communication that divinizes us. We recall his statement that God is both the giver and the gift, indicating that the mystery is not remote but near, closer to us than we are to ourselves.

Our graced condition grounds Rahner's understanding of a universal revelation, a call of God available to all people and heard in that inner sanctuary we call conscience. God's self-giving issues in the explicit normative revelation found in the Bible and handed on in the church. The notion of a universal revelation creates a salvation optimism based on fidelity to conscience that functions as an implicit form of faith. Rahner next turns to Christology, the longest chapter in *Foundations* and the center point of his whole synthesis. Jesus is the model of fulfilled humanity, the best we have produced, the exemplar of what it means to be human. Anthropology finds its fulfillment in Christology. Jesus is the parable of the Father, the fullness of divine revelation. He is the definitive Prophet and the absolute Savior. He is the incarnate Word, the meeting point of divine self-communication and human receptivity. He is so obedient, so open that he is totally filled with the Holy Spirit and is God personally present in our midst. Through his death and resurrection, he conquered death and has become life-giving Spirit for all people in all historical periods and all cultures. The church is the community of faith that keeps alive his memory, celebrates his continuing presence, and carries on his mission to spread the reign of God in the world. The Bible is the book of the church produced by the community of faith. The church actualizes itself through the sacraments and calls all its members to strive for holiness by living out Christ's command to love God and neighbor. The baptized carry out this task with the hope that the deepest longings of the heart will finally be fulfilled in the life of heaven and that the history of the world will ultimately reach its goal when God will be all in all.

Sequence

The sequence of topics in *Foundations* has great pastoral relevance. Starting with human experience is a useful method of prompting reflection on the Christian tradition. The theology of grace sets the stage for attention to ongoing revelation. The centrality of Christ gives focus to the whole Christian message. Discussing the church after Christ helps avoid ecclesiolatry. Treating the Christian life as a combination of charity and worship protects against an unhealthy split between liturgy and life. Considering the Bible within the context of the church grounds a radical critique of fundamentalism. The internal logic of the Rahnerian paradigm appeals to the contemporary mindset and provides a useful framework for pastoral strategies.

Practical Applications

Components of this paradigm are helpful to people I serve. Collegians often resonate with the descriptions of the human drive for love. Individuals dealing with guilt feelings need reminders that God is close and loving. Those who are tempted to religious exclusivism need the message of salvation optimism. Rahner's robust Christology is a helpful corrective to Christians who have reduced Jesus to an ethical teacher. People upset with the institutional church can use a reminder that the church, despite its sinfulness, still mediates Christ and his grace to us. Rahner provides a solid basis for calling for full active participation in the liturgy and for keeping the essential connection between love of God and neighbor. Within this general framework, Rahner helps us see other specific connections: for example, appreciating the assumption of Mary in relation to Christ's saving work and understanding adoration of the Blessed Sacrament as grounded in the communal celebration of the Eucharist. And for all of us, he has a message of hope based not on human accomplishments but on the promises of God who is faithful and trustworthy.

Other Theologians

For me, the Rahnerian paradigm functions as a broad framework open to the perspectives and insights of other theologians. Although his fundamental approach to ministry shapes my pastoral practice, situations often dictate drawing on other theological or secular sources. For example, giving a presentation to a group of women studying Scripture moves me to draw on parts of Elizabeth Johnson's *She Who Is*; participating in a social justice seminar takes me back to

The Theology of Liberation by Gustavo Gutierrez; directing an independent study on the thought of Paul Tillich demands a review of his *Systematic Theology*; preaching a homily on the beauty of Christmas enables me to use ideas from von Balthasar's *The Glory of the Lord*; giving a speech to local business leaders forces me to look at *The Spirit of Democratic Capitalism* by Michael Novak; providing spiritual direction to a graduate student interested in prayer prompts me to look over Thomas Merton's *Contemplative Prayer*. Although I tend to view the work of other theologians through a Rahnerian lens, the great diversity of pastoral tasks seems to dictate for me a more eclectic approach.

Humble Confidence

Finally, pondering all these pastoral responsibilities, I am conscious of the importance of the Rahnerian-inspired dialectical virtue of humble confidence. No one can know all the answers, and so it is quite acceptable to admit ignorance and offer to search for helpful responses. On the other hand, Rahner reminds us that pastors represent a tradition that has much to offer the contemporary world. The strengths of our Catholic tradition are a marvelous corrective to our contemporary sociological and cultural weaknesses. We have a communal sense of human existence that challenges a self-serving individualism; a tradition of asceticism that counters consumerism; a respect for reason, philosophy, and theology that runs counter to strains of anti-intellectualism; an awareness of the mystery dimension of life that subverts superficiality in all its guises; a respect for life in all stages of development that opposes threats to the most vulnerable. Representing the Catholic tradition in today's world is a great honor and demanding responsibility worthy of our best efforts. We do not have all the answers, but we have perspectives and insights that can enrich our culture and improve our society. The virtue of humble confidence, grounded in Rahner's theology, provides great guidance and motivation for all pastoral tasks including teaching, preaching, spiritual direction, comforting the grieving, and celebrating the sacraments. For me, the title of this book, *Humble Confidence*, represents an ideal deeply rooted in the spiritual and pastoral theology of Karl Rahner, paradigm maker and spiritual guide.

Epilogue:
Defending Rahner Against His Critics

Today we hear voices in the Catholic community questioning the continuing relevance of Rahner's theology for the contemporary world. The neoconservative author George Weigel, for example, has claimed that the future of Catholic theology will not be Rahnerian because his writings were too narrowly directed to German academics and do not resonate with the broader Christian audience. Perhaps Weigel had in mind Rahner's philosophical analyses found in *Spirit in the World* and *Hearers of the Word*, or some of his more abstract articles in *Theological Investigations*. Along these same lines, R. R. Reno, the editor of the neoconservative journal *First Things*, has criticized Rahner for failing to cultivate "a theological loyalty to the Church and the magisterium."[1] According to Reno, Rahner's theological project has failed in important ways: to find an integral role for Scripture in theology; to overcome the modern tyranny of relativism; to show the centrality of Jesus as the font of all truth; and to mount an effective critique of contemporary culture that would highlight the hard choices facing Christians today. Thus, Rahner's day has passed, and we must look elsewhere for guidance. Reno suggests we turn to the theology of Joseph Ratzinger who has consistently fought relativism with the clear Gospel-inspired truth of Christ. Furthermore, his theology prompts loyalty to the church and provides a radical critique of contemporary culture. Reno's analysis suggests that a critique of Rahner is part of the neoconservative effort to promote the "reform of the reform" movement espoused by Pope Emeritus Benedict.

Followers of the prolific Swiss theologian Hans Urs von Balthasar, echoing their mentor, criticize Rahner for putting too much emphasis on the universal orientation of all human beings to the Holy Mystery and not enough on the distinctive message of Christianity centered on the concrete historical figure Jesus of Nazareth. In other words, Rahner's transcendental philosophy has overwhelmed his Christology, leaving his whole theological project without a clear focus on Jesus the concrete absolute. This has led to what Robert Barron calls "beige Catholicism,"[2] which does not excite younger Catholics and cannot provide an effective alternative to secular culture.

Liberation theologians of various types have criticized Rahner's anthropology for ignoring the concrete social, economic, and political situations of individuals and classes today. They are concerned about oppressive situations, systemic evil, social sin, and false consciousness—all factors underdeveloped by Rahner. They do not see enough emphasis in Rahner on the theme of liberation found in the Bible, nor on the Christian calling to challenge and transform unjust social structures.

These criticisms suggest, at least, that Rahner's theology does not dominate the Catholic world as it did in the years immediately after the council, when his thought set the framework for much of the discussion in the theological world and informed the spirituality of many Catholics, including those who had no explicit knowledge of him. Today Rahnerians share the theological stage with the Balthasarians and a wide variety of liberationists. Contemporary Catholic spirituality reflects a whole range of influences: Christian classics, popular writers like Dorothy Day and Thomas Merton, Eastern religions, and twelve-step programs. This does not mean, however, that Rahner's theology is passé. On the contrary, it has been enriched and deepened by dialogue with other approaches, making it even more relevant for our pluralistic world.

Rahner's Responses

We recall that Rahner made it very clear to me back in 1977 that he did not take very seriously the criticism that his theology was too abstract and lacked a concrete Christocentric focus. Considering the centrality of Christ in his *Foundations* and the great number of meditations he wrote on the life of Jesus, we can see why he simply dismissed the charge that his philosophy overwhelms his Christology. After admitting that he took seriously the liberationist critique of his theology, he added that his transcendental theology was open to and, in fact, calls for consideration of historical, interpersonal, and societal factors. His summary statement was that theology must be "mystical and political."

Rahner's New Paradigm

One fundamental response to critics who want to dismiss Rahner as irrelevant is that his new theological paradigm is a classic achievement with permanent significance. He now functions like the other great paradigm makers, Origen, Augustine, Aquinas, and Bonaventure, who have continued to enrich Catholic theology even in changing circumstances. It is true that Rahner refocused the Catholic theological tradition in dialogue with modernity, but our postmodern world continues to be influenced by modern movements such as the Enlightenment and secular humanism. His continuing relevance is also enhanced by the great variety of his dialogue partners: Ignatian spirituality, the Catholic mystical tradition, scholastic theology, the Eastern fathers, enlightenment rationalism, modern atheism, Marxist philosophy, modern science, existential philosophy, the ecumenical movement, and many others. In our fragmented culture, we can continue to benefit from Rahner's presentation of the Christian faith as a whole, as an integrated symbol system, which speaks to the deepest longings of the human heart. Given the challenge of integrating the knowledge explosion, Christians need a way of seeing how the various areas of theology fit together organically. As we have noted, his theological anthropology contains seeds of his doctrine of God. His theology of grace provides the basis and framework for a contemporary understanding of salvation and revelation. For him, Christology, which is at the center of his theological synthesis, is the fulfillment of anthropology and presents Jesus as the definitive revelation of God's saving love. The church is the sacrament of the risen Christ, the People of God called to celebrate the seven sacraments and to live Christ's command to love God and neighbor. Christians live in eschatological hope for the ultimate success of the evolutionary process and the complete fulfillment of the deepest longings of the human heart. The organic character of Rahner's paradigm can serve as an enduring model of how Christians can see their faith as a consistent whole and therefore cope better with a rapidly changing world.

Method of Correlation

Furthermore, Rahner's method of correlation, which calls for a mutually enriching dialogue with the contemporary world, remains one of the most sophisticated methods of relating the Christian tradition to any and all developments in society and culture. This means that Rahner's theology, framed in dialogue with the modern world, can still speak to our electronic postmodern world, which is post-patriarchal, postcolonial, postindustrial, post–Cold War, and post-denominational. His methodology encourages dialogue on postmodern issues such as globalization and the new tribalism, gender relations, interreligious collaboration, and international relations. The Rahnerian paradigm does not directly deal with all these issues, but it does provide a framework for further thought and motivation for continuing dialogue.

Current Influence

Important Catholic theologians today continue to draw on Rahner's theology for seminal insights and practical wisdom. Elizabeth Johnson, to take a prime example, in her popular book *Quest for the Living God*, devotes twenty pages to Rahner's doctrine of God and cites him in a number of other places, more than any other author. In the United States, the Karl Rahner Society, founded in 1981 to keep his thought alive, hosts meetings at the annual convention of the Catholic Theological Society of America and publishes articles on Rahner in the Marquette University Journal *Philosophy Theology*. Younger scholars continue to write dissertations on some aspect of Rahner's theology, and some of them have explicitly tried to refute the claim that Rahner is no longer relevant. Rahner's continuing influence extends beyond the Catholic community. For instance, the Lutheran historian Martin

Marty, in his 2007 book *The Mystery of the Child*, drew heavily on Rahner's 1962 article on "Ideas for a Theology of Childhood." This is typical of the way authors continue to find nuggets of wisdom in Rahner's vast corpus and creatively relate these insights to contemporary issues.

Rahner's Spiritual Perspective

Karl Rahner's wide-ranging writings on the spiritual life, selectively noted in this book, provide a strong response to the neoconservative criticism and suggest an enduring role for his theology in the decades ahead. It is indeed possible to read many of his academic articles in *Theological Investigations* and wonder if his thought resonates with a popular audience. It is hard to read his prayers in *Encounters with Silence*, however, and fail to find descriptions that touch the heart as well as the head. A critic could peruse certain parts of *Foundations of Christian Faith* and come to the conclusion (mistaken, I am convinced) that Rahner's transcendental philosophy has overwhelmed the particularity of the Gospel message. But it is hard to imagine an honest searcher prayerfully engaging Rahner's homilies in *The Great Church Year* without recognizing his profoundly Christocentric piety. The spiritual writings of Rahner reveal the wellspring of his whole theology and highlight the dynamic interplay between his philosophy of human existence and the concrete particularity of Christianity. In this mutual exchange, the Gospel remains norm and judge, as Rahner explicitly affirmed and consistently practiced.

Theology and Spirituality

Rahner made an enduring contribution to the spiritual quest in the twenty-first century by insisting on the organic unity between theology and spirituality. In his own time, he clearly recognized the great dangers of the "rift, all too common, even today, between lived piety and abstract theology."[3] Those dangers are intensified in the postmodern world, which celebrates multiple perspectives and fosters superficial and faddish approaches to spirituality. Furthermore, we have witnessed the growth of a distinct academic discipline called "spirituality," which should engage systematic theology as a primary dialogue partner but often fails to do so. Rahner's whole theological enterprise can be seen as an effort to bridge the gap between spirituality, broadly conceived as lived experience guided by the Spirit, and the academic work of professional theologians. He had great confidence that theology, true to its nature and calling, would help people achieve a closer personal relationship to Christ. For Rahner, theology has the explicit task of correlating the Christian tradition and contemporary experience. It must show how Scripture guides the human adventure and how specific Christian doctrines illumine the significant questions of the day.

Rahner's Spiritual Writings

The claim that Rahner's theology is spiritually relevant is most evident in his prayers and homilies. He himself thought that his small book *On Prayer* contained some of his most practical theological insights. For example, he presents a reinterpreted theology of grace as the basis for making our everyday life itself a prayer so that we can transform the "soul-killing monotony" of mundane tasks into praise of God and love of neighbor, which will lead to greater inner peace. According to Rahner, "We cannot find a better means for growing spiritually than through our everyday life."[4]

When I teach graduate theology courses on Rahner's spirituality, I have the students read his *Foundations of Christian Faith*, which provides a solid basis and broad perspective for discussing contemporary spiritual issues. When I present this same material to adult learners, I have them read, instead of *Foundations*, excerpts from Rahner's spiritual writings that contain his fundamental theological insights expressed in more concrete language with more obvious applications to the spiritual journey. My list of recommended spiritual books by Rahner include: *The Great Church Year; Biblical Homilies; The Spiritual Exercises; Encounters with Silence; Watch and Pray with Me; The Eternal Year; On Prayer; Opportunities for Faith; Christians at the Crossroads; Belief Today; Leading a Christian Life; The Priesthood; Everyday Faith; Mary, Mother of the Lord; The Religious Life Today; Allow Yourself to Be Forgiven; The Courage to Pray; Meditations on Freedom and the Spirit; Prayers for a Lifetime;* and volumes 3, 7, 8, and 16 of his *Theological Investigations.*

Rahner's Influence in Asia

Around the Pacific Rim today there is interest in Rahner's theology, as indicated in the book *Rahner Beyond Rahner: A Great Theologian Encounters the Pacific Rim*, published in 2005. Rahner himself did not visit Asian countries and did not participate in direct dialogue with Eastern religious traditions. Moreover, his comments about other religions at times lack depth and precision. Nevertheless, important theologians currently engaged in interfaith dialogue find that Rahner provides a firm and broad theological framework that is open to the truth, goodness, and beauty found in other religious traditions. His much criticized notion of the anonymous Christian enables Christian scholars to detect the presence of divine grace in the teachings and practices of other religions, while maintaining the centrality of Christ as the prime mediator of saving grace. In China, for example, the University of Renmin in Beijing has hosted courses and conferences on Rahner's theology offered by American scholars. A Chinese graduate student recently completed a doctorate at Innsbruck on Rahner's early philosophical works. Chinese scholars have shown an interest in Rahner's anonymous Christian notion as a way of staying open to Christianity without considering all aspects of it as a foreign import. Some Chinese intellectuals who recognize the need for a socially responsible spirituality in their rapidly changing country have expressed interest in Rahner's transcendental anthropology, which has meaning for them despite its cultural context so different from their own.

Various contributors to *Rahner Beyond Rahner* have noted other ways his theology can enrich the contemporary religious dialogue in the Pacific Rim. Rahner's theology of the cross can speak to the great problems of human suffering in that part of the world. His ecclesiology, which openly acknowledges the sinfulness of the church, can help Asian Catholics, living as a minority in most countries, deal with the sex abuse crisis and other church failures. Finally, Rahner's doctrine of God, which insists that the divine mystery is ultimately inexpressible and incomprehensible, opens the way for dialogue with Buddhists who prefer silence on questions of ultimacy. On a personal note, a number of years ago at an annual meeting of the Catholic Theological Society of America, I encountered a small group of Asiatic graduate students who had studied Rahner's theology. When they found out that I knew Rahner personally, they excitedly asked many questions about him as a person. It was my first clue that Rahner's influence was spreading to the Asian world.

All this anecdotal material does not amount to a great Rahnerian groundswell in the Asian world, but it does suggest that his influence is expanding in unexpected ways that may bear greater fruit in the decades ahead. Once again we see that Rahner's theology, far from dead, retains the power to produce fruitful dialogue with great spiritual and pastoral significance.

Selected Bibliography

Books by Karl Rahner

Belief Today. New York: Sheed and Ward, 1967.

Biblical Homilies. New York: Herder and Herder, 1967.

The Christian Commitment: Essays in Pastoral Theology. Translated by Cecily Hastings. New York: Sheed and Ward, 1963.

Encounters with Silence. Westminster, MD: Newman Press, 1960.

The Eternal Year. Baltimore, MD: Helicon, 1964.

Everyday Faith. Translated by W. J. O'Hara. New York: Herder and Herder, 1968.

Foundations of Christian Faith: An Introduction to the Idea of Christianity. Translated by William V. Dych. New York: Seabury Press, 1978.

The Great Church Year: The Best of Rahner's Homilies, Sermons and Meditations. Edited by Albert Raffelt. New York: Crossroad, 1993.

The Love of Jesus and the Love of Neighbor. Translated by Robert Barr. New York: Crossroad, 1983.

Meditations of the Sacraments. New York: Seabury Press, 1977.

On Prayer. New York: Paulist Press, 1968.

The Parish from Theology to Practice. Edited by Hugo Rahner. Translated by Robert Kress. Westminster, MD: Newman Press, 1958.

Prayers & Meditations: An Anthology of the Spiritual Writings of Karl Rahner. Edited by John Griffiths. New York: Seabury Press, 1980.

Prayers for a Lifetime. New York: Crossroad, 1984.

The Shape of the Church to Come. New York: Seabury Press, 1974.

Spirit in the World. Translated by William Dych. New York: Herder and Herder, 1968. Abbr. *Spirit*.

Spiritual Exercises. New York: Herder and Herder, 1965.

Theological Investigations, vols. 1–23. Vols. 1–6 published in Baltimore by Helicon. Vols. 7–10 in New York by Herder and Herder. Vols. 11–14 in New York by Seabury Press. 1961–1976. Vols. 15–23 in New York by Crossroad.

The Trinity. London: Burns and Oates, 1967.

Other Authors

Bacik, James. *Apologetics and the Eclipse of Mystery: Mystagogy According to Karl Rahner*. Notre Dame, IN: University of Notre Dame Press, 1980.

Bacik, James, and Kevin Anderson. *A Light Unto My Path: Crafting Effective Homilies*. Mahwah, NJ: Paulist Press, 2006.

Baron, Robert. *The Strangest Way: Walking the Christian Path*. Maryknoll, NY: Orbis Books, 2002.

Being and Truth: Essays in Honour of John Macquarrie. Edited by Alistair Kee and Eugene Thomas Long. London: SCM Press, 1986.

MABDA. *A Common Word between Us and You: Five-Year Anniversary Edition*. Amman, Jordan: Royal Aal Al-Bayt Institute for Islamic Thought, 2012.

Models of God and Alternative Ultimate Realities. Edited by Jeanine Diller and Asa Kasher. New York: Springer, 2013.

Mother Teresa: Come Be My Light: The Private Writings of the Saint of Calcutta. Edited by Brian Kolodiejchuk. New York: Image, 2009.

Rahner Beyond Rahner: A Great Theologian Encounters the Pacific Rim. Edited by Paul Crowley. Lanham, MD: Sheed and Ward, 2005.

Notes

Chapter 1 (pages 1–19)

1. For the importance of Rahner's early faith development, see James Bacik, *Apologetics and the Eclipse of Mystery: Mystagogy According to Karl Rahner* (Notre Dame, IN: University of Notre Dame Press, 1980), 48.

2. For an English translation, see Karl Rahner, "The Spiritual Senses According to Origen," in *Theological Investigations 16* (New York: Crossroad, 1979), 81–103.

3. See Karl Rahner, "The Doctrine of the Spiritual Senses in the Middle Ages," in *Theological Investigations 16*, 104–34.

4. Karl Rahner, "The Concept of Existential Philosophy in Heidegger," trans. Andew Tallon, *Philosophy Today* 13, no. 2 (1969): 126–37.

5. Karl Rahner, *Spirit in the World*, trans. William Dych (New York: Herder and Herder, 1968), 407.

6. For a more extensive treatment of the Rahner existentials, see James J. Bacik, "Rahner's Anthropology: The Basis for a Dialectical Spirituality," in *Being and Truth: Essays in Honour of John Macquarrie*, ed. Alistair Kee and Eugene Thomas Long (London: SCM Press, 1986), 168–82.

7. Rahner, *Spirit in the World*, 407.

8. *Prayers and Meditations: An Anthology of the Spiritual Writings of Karl Rahner*, ed. John Griffiths (New York: Seabury Press, 1980).

9. Karl Rahner, *The Love of Jesus and the Love of Neighbor*, trans. Robert Barr (New York: Crossroad, 1983).

Chapter 2 (pages 21–42)

1. For a more scholarly treatment of the material in this chapter, see James Bacik, "Karl Rahner on God" in *Models of God and Alternative Ultimate Realities*, ed. Jeanine Diller and Asa Kasher (New York: Springer, 2013), 441–51.

2. This and the following sections up to and including "Finding God in the World" are summaries of Rahner's *Foundations of Christian Faith*, trans. William V. Dych (New York: Seabury Press, 1978). See especially chap. 2, 44–89.

3. Ibid., 48.

4. Ibid., 51.

5. Ibid., 51–57.

6. Ibid., 63.

7. Ibid., 68–71.

8. Ibid., 70.

9. Ibid., 71–75.

10. Ibid., 75–81.

11. Ibid., 81–89.

12. Ibid., 83.

13. Ibid., 89.

14. For one of Rahner's seminal articles on grace, see "Some Implications of the Scholastic Concept of Uncreated Grace," in *Theological Investigations 1* (New York: Crossroad, 1973), 322–44.

15. For an analysis of grace and consciousness, see Karl Rahner, "Religious Enthusiasm and the Experience of Grace," in *Theological Investigations 16* (New York: Crossroad, 1979), 36–51.

16. For a summary of Rahner's notion of mystagogy, see James Bacik, *Apologetics and the Eclipse of Mystery: Mystagogy According to Karl Rahner* (Notre Dame, IN: University of Notre Dame Press, 1980).

17. Rahner, *Foundations*, 22.

18. Karl Rahner, *On Prayer* (New York: Paulist Press, 1968), 24–27.

19. Karl Rahner, *Prayers for a Lifetime* (New York: Crossroad, 1984), 8–15.

20. Ibid., 40–42.

21. Karl Rahner, *Belief Today* (New York: Sheed and Ward, 1967), 39–40.

22. For a Rahnerian approach to preaching, see James Bacik and Kevin Anderson, *A Light Unto My Path: Crafting Effective Homilies* (Mahwah, NJ: Paulist Press, 2006).

23. For Rahner's fundamental approach to the topic, see *The Trinity* (London: Burns and Oates, 1967).

24. Rahner, *The Trinity*, 23.

25. Karl Rahner, *The Eternal Year* (Baltimore, MD: Helicon, 1964), 44.

26. Rahner, *Prayers for a Lifetime*, 17–18.

Chapter 3 (pages 43–70)

1. For Rahner's approach to the history of Jesus, see *Foundations of Christian Faith*, trans. William V. Dych (New York: Seabury Press, 1978), 228–64.

2. For Rahner's defense of the true humanity of Jesus, see "Christology Today," in *Theological Investigations 17* (New York: Crossroad, 1981), 24–38.

3. For elements of Rahner's transcendental Christology in various parts of his *Foundations*, see *Foundations* 178–203; 206–12; 212–28; 298–302.

4. For Rahner's theology of the death and resurrection of Jesus, see *Foundations*, 265–85.

5. Karl Rahner, *Everyday Faith*, trans. W. J. O'Hara (New York: Herder and Herder, 1968), 76–83.

6. Ibid., 80ff.

7. Rahner, *Foundations*, 284.

8. Ibid.

9. Although Rahner himself was a limited participant in interreligious dialogue, his theology set the stage for others. See "The Importance of the Non-Christian Religions for Salvation," in *Theological Investigations 18* (New York: Crossroad, 1983), 288–95.

10. Karl Rahner, *The Love of Jesus and the Love of Neighbor*, trans. Robert Barr (New York: Crossroad, 1983), 23.

11. Ibid., 22.

12. Ibid.

13. The quotations from this section are taken from Rahner's *Spiritual Exercises* (New York: Herder and Herder, 1965), 146–50.

14. Ibid., 151–60.

15. Ibid., 163–68.

16. The quotations from this section are taken from Rahner's *The Great Church Year: The Best of Rahner's Homilies, Sermons and Meditations*, ed. Albert Raffelt (New York: Crossroad, 1993), 238–39.

17. Rahner, *Spiritual Exercises*, 169–78.

18. Rahner, *The Great Church Year*, 267–69.

19. Ibid., 340–42.

20. The quotations from this section are taken from Rahner's *Biblical Homilies* (New York: Herder and Herder, 1967), 45–49.

21. Ibid., 72–75.

22. The quotations from this section are taken from Rahner's *Meditations on the Sacraments* (New York: Seabury Press, 1977), 29–41.

23. Rahner, *Spiritual Exercises*, 217–26.

24. Ibid., 227–28.

25. Ibid., 228–29.

26. Ibid., 229–31.

27. Ibid., 231–33.

28. Ibid., 234–43.

29. Ibid., 244–50.

30. The quotations from this section are taken from Rahner's *The Eternal Year* (Baltimore, MD: Helicon, 1964), 97–104.

Chapter 4 (pages 71–91)

1. For an overview of Rahner's ecclesiology, see *Foundations of Christian Faith*, trans. William V. Dych (New York: Seabury Press, 1978), 322–401.

2. For this connection, see Karl Rahner, "Courage for an Ecclesial Christianity," in *Concern for the Church: Theological Investigations 20* (New York: Crossroad, 1981), 3–12.

3. Rahner, "The Basic Theological Interpretation of the Second Vatican Council," in *Concern for the Church: Theological Investigations 20*, 77–89.

4. Ibid.

5. Karl Rahner, "The Theology of the Parish," in *The Parish from Theology to Practice*, ed. Hugo Rahner, trans. Robert Kress (Westminster, MD: Newman Press, 1958), 30.

6. Quotations from this section are from Rahner's *The Shape of the Church to Come* (New York: Seabury Press, 1974), 29–34.

7. Ibid., 38–42.

8. Ibid., 56–60.

9. Ibid., 61–63.

10. Ibid., 71–75.

11. Ibid., 93–101.

12. Ibid., 82–89.

13. Ibid., 102–7.

14. Ibid., 108–18.

15. For Rahner's argument in favor of women's ordination, see "Women and the Priesthood," in *Concern for the Church: Theological Investigations 20*, 35–47.

16. Expanding on Rahner's ideas, this section makes concrete applications to pastoral leadership in the United States today.

Chapter 5 (pages 93–163)

1. For the last thirty-six years I have written a monthly "Reflections" article distributed privately to friends and anyone interested. Dealing with a broad range of church and secular issues, they are an extension of my pastoral ministry and reflect Rahner's influence on various aspects of my service as a priest.

2. Karl Rahner, *Prayers for a Lifetime* (New York: Crossroad, 1984), 144–49.

3. Karl Rahner, *Foundations of Christian Faith*, trans. William V. Dych (New York: Seabury Press, 1978), 284.

4. Mother Teresa and Brian Kolodiejchuk, *Mother Teresa: Come Be My Light: The Private Writings of the Saint of Calcutta* (New York: Image, 2009), 14.

5. Ibid., 15.

6. Ibid., 14.

7. Ibid., 24.

8. Ibid., 25.

9. Ibid., 28.

10. Ibid., 40.

11. Ibid., 44.

12. Ibid., 99.

13. Ibid., 187.

14. Ibid.

15. Ibid.

16. Ibid., 192.

17. Ibid., 217.

18. MABDA, *A Common Word between Us and You: Five-Year Anniversary Edition* (Amman, Jordan: Royal Aal Al-Bayt Institute for Islamic Thought, 2012), 53.

Epilogue (pages 165–72)

1. R. R. Reno, "Rahner the Restorationist," *First Things*, no. 233 (May 2013): 45–51.

2. Robert Barron, *The Strangest Way: Walking the Christian Path* (Maryknoll, NY: Orbis Books, 2002), 12.

3. Karl Rahner, *Theological Investigations 16*, trans. David Morland (New York: Crossroad, 1979), 72.

4. Karl Rahner, *On Prayer* (New York: Paulist Press, 1968), 53.

Index

soteriology, 51–52, 109
soul, 9, 11, 20, 27, 49, 60, 61, 69, 72, 97,
    98, 108, 124–26, 148–50, 155
Source, 5, 10, 14, 22, 24, 31, 33, 34, 37,
    39, 41, 42, 47, 48, 54, 55, 70, 99, 137,
    154, 160–61
Spirit in the World, 4–5, 6, 7, 15–16, 165
Spiritual Big Bang, 135–38
Spiritual Exercises, 1, 2, 54, 170
"spiritual father" model, 103–6
supernatural, 24, 28, 156, 158, 159
supernatural existential, 3
Synoptic Gospels, 43, 46, 127

T
Teilhard de Chardin, 111
Teresa of Avila, 154
Theism, 24, 111, 151–55
Theology for Renewal, 93
Theology of Liberation, The, 163
Thomas the Twin, 67, 68
Tillich, Paul, 111, 151, 163
"transcendental Christology," 47, 48

Transfiguration, x, 44, 59–60, 64
trinitarian monotheism, 34
Trinity, 21, 27, 33–34, 35
tritheism, 34

U
uncreated grace, 27
Unitatis Redintegratio, 77
Updike, John, 155–59

V
Vatican II. *See* Second Vatican Council
Volf, Miroslav, 97

W
Wedding Feast of Cana, 58
Weigel, George, 116, 165
Wittgenstein, Ludwig, 23
world church, x, 76–80
World War II, 82, 104

Y
Yahweh, 56, 65, 151